ALSACE

Tourist guide with more than 200 colour photographs and detailed maps, as well as specially selected gastronomic tips

Text: Marie-Christine Périllon
Photos: Roger Rothan/Airdiasol

Kraichgau Verlag GmbH

Contents

Such a special little part of France

Alsace is the smallest region in France as regards area, but the most highly populated as regards density. Alsace has 1734000 inhabitants -209 inhabitants per km2, whereas the average number of inhabitants per km2 in metropolitan France is 108.

This is by no means the only peculiarity of this region which looks back on a long and eventful history. The health insurance regime, the right to hunt and the concordat regime of the churches are among these "Alsatian exceptions". Linguists distinguish between twenty-five different regions of dialect in the two départements of the lower Rhine. It is enough to hear someone from Mulhouse conversing with someone from Strasbourg to notice the notorious differences in pronunciation and accent. This diversity is reflected in the cooking where the fleischnacke (rolled and stuffed meat) are considered to be even more a speciality of the Higher Rhine that the tartes flambées from the Lower Rhine.

Alsace has preserved much of its rich history. Most of the main roads that cross Alsace were created by the Romans, who, after the Celts, were the first to occupy this region. Few reliefs dating back to this time still remain on the surface, all having been carefully preserved in museums. On the other hand, the Middle Ages and the Renaissance left their mark on all Alsatian towns and villages, which have peppered the urban countryside with their opulent hotels, their churches with a skilful mixture of Romanesque and Gothic art and their curved half-timbered houses. Alsace was one of the cradles of Humanism and of printing, which, via the "intermediary" of the Rhine and its tributaries, propagated to all the neighbouring countries. The 15th Century was that of the Protestant Reformation which was spread by great preachers such as Martin Bucer and Jean Calvin. As a result of the Treaty of Westphalia in 1648, Alsace progressively entered into the hands of the French. It is from this period that the profusion of French hotels originates, which gradually came to vie with the half-timbered homes. And the pink sandstone of the dressed stone buildings began to merge with the dark wood of the white or coloured daub houses, creating a new harmony which didn't mar the old. A region of contrasts, Alsace has always managed to integrate brand-new ideas, adapting them in its own special way. The whole of Alsace is characterised by this synthesis, which, from the architecture to the cooking, as well as the arts, defines the local spirit. Unsurprisingly, its sights attract many tourists: Strasbourg Cathedral, the Unterlinden à Colmar Museum and Haut-Koenigsbourg Fortress, nowadays followed by both the Ecomusée d'Ungersheim and the Musée de l'Automobile de

Mulhouse [Mulhouse Automobile Museum] in terms of visitor numbers, all of which are among the most popular sites in France.

Whether they are called route des églises romanes, route des châteaux-forts, route des Crêtes, route du Sundgau, route de la Carpe Frite, route du Tabac, Route des Vins or route de Choucroute, all of the trips are highly educational, especially when they are combined with a visit to Alsace's museums. These traditional itineraries can be complemented with visits to industrial sites, such as the hydroelectric dams along the Rhine, the brewing factories, and those that produce food, textiles or cars, or even those of the former silver and potash mines, which make the region appear economically prosperous. However, the most symbolic visit is to the European Council. Created in 1949 with ten member states, this institution today has 47 members. The European Parliament was founded in 1958 as a result of the Treaty of Roman and currently has a total of 785 members representing 492 million inhabitants. Situated opposite the European district of Strasbourg, these two institutions are the guarantors of a more democratic and a more united Europe, whilst a little further along the Rhine, the construction of a bridge between France and Germany is in the process of reaching completion.

The stork, the emblematic bird of Alsace, is no longer in danger of extinction of its

species in the region. Several stork reintroduction centres ensure the bird's survival.

Dates

From the 7th Century B.C. Alsace was inhabited by the Celts.

58 B.C.:	Julius Caesar defeats Arioviste in the region of Mulhouse, integrating this region into the Roman world.
12 B.C.:	Creation of the Argentoratum military camp, which is to become Strasbourg
Around 70:	Creation of two provinces of Germania Inferior (Cologne) and Superior (Mayence) which includes Alsace.
451:	Invasion of Attila. End of Alemannic occupation of Alsace. Destruction of Argentoratum
496:	Victory of Clovis against the Alemanni at Tolbiac and settlement of the Franks in part of Alsace
640-740:	Alsace forms a duchy. Foundation of monasteries under the Etichonids.
842:	The Strasbourg Oaths unite the heirs of Charlemagne, Louis the German and Charles the Bald, against their brother Lothar
870:	Treaty of Meersen which assigns Alsace to Louis the German
1049-1054:	Bruno d'Eguisheim becomes pope under the name of Leon IX

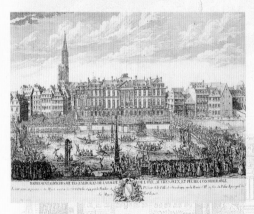

Representation of the parties held by the city of Strasbourg in honour of the visit of Louis XV (1744)

1273:	Rudolph of Hapsburg becomes Emperor. This is the beginning of Austrian Alsace, which lasts until 1648.
1354:	Foundation of the Decapole, league of ten imperial towns.
1434-1444:	Gutenberg to Strasbourg
1469-1474:	Burgundian attempt of annexation of Alsace.
1521:	Beginning of Protestantism in Alsace
1525:	Peasants' War
1555:	The Peace of Augsburg settles the borders between Catholic and Protestant seigneuries.

1618-1648:	The Thirty Years' War rages
1648:	The Treaty of Westphalia: French troops settle in Alsace
1675:	Victory of Turenne against the imperial forces just before Turckheim
1681:	Annexation of Strasbourg which becomes a "free royal city"
1744:	Great festivities held in honour of Louis XV's visit to Strasbourg
1798:	Reunion of Mulhouse to France after a vote of the bourgeoisie

Portrait of Leon IX

1815:	Due to the Treaty of Vienna, Alsace loses Landau and sees its Northern border shifted to the Lauter.
1870:	Franco-Prussian War. Battles of Wissembourg and Froeschwiller. Siege of Strasbourg
1871:	Due to the Treaty of Frankfurt, Alsace becomes "Reichsland", land of the Empire.
1911:	Establishment of a constitution for Alsace-Lorraine and election of the diet (Landtag/state parliament)
1915:	Battles of Hartmannswillerkopf' (Old Germany) and of Le Linge.
Nov. 1918:	Return to France
1925-1935:	Construction of the Maginot Line
Sept. 1939:	Beginning of the Second World War and evacuation of a third of the population to South-East France
25 August 1942:	130,000 Alsatians and Moselle citizens join the German army
Nov. 1944- March 1945:	Liberation of Alsace by the French troops
1949:	Foundation of the Council of Europe in Strasbourg
1973:	The first Regional Council of Alsace is set up
1979:	Election of the first European Parliament set up in Strasbourg
1992:	With 65% of votes in favour, Alsace is the French region which most supports the Maastricht Agreement

DE L OYE, AUTRES JEUX, ET PECHE CONSIDERABLE

1 Wissembourg

Wissembourg, whose name means white castle, has preserved a very rich heritage. The town dates back to the 6th Century, when King Dagobert built a monastery on the banks of the Lauter River. This was subsequently converted into a Benedictine abbey, the sole remains of which are l'église Saints Pierre et Paul [the Saint Peter and Paul Church], Alsace's largest Gothic building after Strasbourg cathedral. The Romanesque square steeple (1075) constitutes the oldest part of the church, which was entirely recon-

Aerial view of Wissembourg which has preserved more than 70 houses dating back to before 1700.

Information

Wissembourg Tourist Office
9, place de la République, BP 80120, F-67163 Wissembourg cedex
Tel: 33(0)3 88 94 10 11, Fax: 33(0)3 88 94 18 82
in@foot-wissembourg.fr, www.ot-wissembourg.fr
Westercamp Museum, *3, rue du Musée. Tel: 33(0)3 88 54 28 14*
Visiting hours: contact us. A very beautiful Christmas Market.

The Saint Peter and Paul Church, Alsace's largest Gothic church after Strasbourg Cathedral.

The Wissembourg Christ, Alsace's oldest figurative stained-glass window (11th Century) preserved at the Musée de l'Oeuvre Notre-Dame de Strasbourg.
[12] The 15th Century maison du Sel, Wissembourg's most amazing house due to its huge roof.

structed in the 13th Century. It illustrates a harmonious meeting of art from the Rhineland and Champagne region. With its large rose window and its three-bay porch, the south side outshines the main façade. On the north side, there is a cloister with 14th Century trefoil archways from which a door leads to the chapel with six columns which are still adorned with cubic Romanesque cornices. The inside of Saint Peter and Paul displays five-nave architecture, remarkable stained-glass windows and a fresco 11m in height, representing St. Christopher, the tallest character to appear on a French painting. In the North transept, above the organ, is the oldest stained-glass window: Virgin with child, which dates back to 1150.

Close to the church, the old 18th Century Du Doyenné hotel houses the subprefecture. Not far from the former hospital, today a retirement home, was the residence of the King of Poland, Stanislas Leszczinski, during his time in exile. His daughter, Marie, married King Louis XV in 1725. One

The 15th Century maison du Sel [House of Salt], whose claim to fame is its huge roof.

of Wissembourg's most spectacular residences is the maison du Sel (1448) [House of Salt], which was first a hospital, then a salt depot and then an abattoir. On the banks of the Lauter, you will find the Ancienne Couronne [Old Crown], which dates back to 1491. Close by, a painted façade identifies the maison Vogelsberger from 1540. The red sandstone town hall, built in the 18th Century by Joseph Massol, stands on the place de la République. On the sundial, a Latin inscription: "In the reign of Louis XV I rose from my ashes", refers to the fire which ravaged the former town hall in 1677. It is also

This house, dating from 1550, provided part of the film setting for "Friend Fritz", based on the novel by Erckmann-Chatrian.

worth a walk behind l'église Saint-Jean [Church of St John], where Martin Bucer preached the Reformation, and a visit to the Westercamp Museum, with its large collection of furniture, costumes and printed artwork.

You can walk from there to the ramparts and the Bruch district quayside enclosed by the 13th Century city walls. It is here that "L'Ami Fritz" ["Friend Fritz"], based on the novel by Erckmann-Chatrian, was filmed in 1932, in the first house decorated with a bay window, on the corner of the quai de Bitche. Other interesting houses line the streets: in fact, Wissembourg boasts more than 70 houses which date back to before 1700.

Restaurant de l'Ange
2, rue de la République
tél: 03 88 94 12 11
Hôtel "Au Moulin de la Walk"
2, rue de la Walk · tél: 03 88 94 06 44

A romantic vision of the district "Le Schlupf", bordered by picturesque houses and with the steeple of the Saint Peter and Paul Church in the background.

2 Lembach, Maginot Line, Fleckenstein Château

The town of Lembach offers a round walk enabling you to discover its heritage. The 14th Century fortified protestant temple has a beautiful 18th Century pulpit which is decorated with a tree of good and evil. It is recommended that you take the Woerth route to visit the Ouvrage du Four à Chaux [Lime Kiln Fortification], which is situated about 1 km away and buried 25 metres deep. One of the Maginot Line's most important fortifications, built between 1930 and 1936, this has preserved its 4 km underground network which

Remains of the Maginot Line: the Ouvrage du Four à Chaux [Lime Kiln Fortification].

Worth a visit: 4 km underground network with six combat blocks.

Information

Lembach and Region Tourist Office 23, Ruote de Bitche, F-67510 Lembach, Tel: 33(0)3 88 94 43 16 – Fax: 33(0)3 88 94 20 04 info@ot-lembach.com; www.ot-lembach.com, **Ouvrage du Four à Chaux – Maginot Line.** www.lignemaginot.com, Fleckenstein Château, Fleckenstein Site, F-67510 Lembach, Tel: 33(0)3 88 94 28 52 info@fleckenstein.fr; www.fleckenstein.fr, Group guided tours of the town and these two monuments are organised the whole year round.

Fleckenstein Château, close to the German border, stands on a rock more than twenty metres above the ground, its impressive pink sandstone silhouette blending in with the huge forest of fir trees.

includes six combat bocks, a power station, an artesian well, eclipse gun turrets, etc… A small museum presents the weapons, the uniforms and posters of the period. The fortification was violently bombed by the Stukas in June of 1940, without however being captured. Restored, it opened its doors to the public in 1983. Overlooking the plain of the Haute Sauer Valley, Fleckenstein is one of the North Vosges' most spectacular châteaux. Built in the 12th Century on a 43 metre-high rock by Emperor Friedrich Barbarossa who entrusted it to his vassal, Gottfried von Fleckenstein, this fortress was reputed to be impregnable. Like many others, the château was razed to the ground in 1680 by Monclar, a general of Louis XIV. There remains a well-preserved entrance door, rooms carved out of the sandstone, one of which houses a small museum, a turret with an emblazoned door, an extraordinary straight staircase cut out of the side of the rock, an exposed part, a part in a tunnel and a part on the upper terrace, the remains of the 13th Century stately home. Close by, on an isolated rock, a 48-step helical staircase leads to a platform with an overall view of the château and the surrounding countryside.

Du Cheval Blanc Inn
(Gastronomic)
4, rue de Wissembourg
Tel: +33388944186

3 Niederbronn-les-Bains

As its name suggests, Nieder-bronn-les-Bains is a spa town whose origins date back to the Romans, who used the healing properties of its waters from the year 48 B.C. The 18°C Roman spring

A spa, the existence of which has been known since the Roman era.

Niederbronn-les-Bains and Region Tourist Office
6, place de l'Hôtel de Ville, F-67110 Niederbronn-les-Bains
Tel: 33(0)3 88 80 89 70, Fax 33(0)3 88 80 37 01
office@niederbronn.com, www.niederbronn.com
North Vosges House of Archaeology, *44, Avenue Foch, Tel: 33(0)3 88 80 36 37*

gushes through the heart of the town under a pavilion in front of the casino. Its healing powers are recommended for osteoarthritis and rheumatism. The Celtic spring, which has a very low mineral content, is used for table water. It has been marketed since 1989 and the bottling factories are open to visitors. However, it is also possible to taste the water directly from its source, which runs through the entrance to the town. It was the Dietrich family, famous industrialists in the region, who contributed to the spa town's development in the 18th Century. Today, Niederbronn has a casino. This spa of the North Vosges Nature Park is also an excellent starting point for several walks, in particular along the châteaux route. At 586 m, nearby Winterberg constitutes the highest point of the North Vosges. An observation post built by the Vosges Club in 1890 enables one to enjoy a beautiful panorama of the surrounding countryside. In addition, a visit to the Maison de l'Archéologie des Vosges du Nord

An overall view of the casino and park, a calm retreat.

The "Lichteneck" Celtic spring is used for table water.

The Roman spring gushes through the heart of the town.

[North Vosges House of Archaeology] is highly recommended. This contains the results of excavations carried out in the region, which was a bastion of the Roman occupation. A whole section is dedicated to the history of fortified châteaux. On leaving Niederbronn, on an Eastern hill, there is a Germany war cemetery from the 1939/1945 War.

Over 15,000 graves of German soldiers that fell in the region during the Second World War are gathered here.

Hôtel-Restaurant du Parc, *Place des Thermes, F-67110 Niederbronn-les-Bains Tel: 33(0)3 88 80 84 84* **Restaurant Les Acacias,** *35 rue des Acacias. Tel: 33(0)3 88 09 00 47*

Falkenstein

Built in the 12th Century, Falkenstein or "falcon rock" was destroyed by a fire in the 16th Century, then rebuilt and damaged by the Thirty Years' War, before being demolished in 1680. One can still make out rooms carved out of the rock, two doors and the remains of a tower. Legend has it that a cooper sometimes comes to strike as many blows at midnight as there will be barrels of wine during the year. On the other side of the hill remain traces of the Helfenstein château.

The châteaux route makes up North Alsace's picturesque round walks.

Windstein

The two Windstein châteaux stand 500 metres apart and were destroyed in 1676 by Montclar, one of Louis XIV's generals who appears to have been a specialist in the demolition of fortified châteaux. The sole remains are some traces of the Vieux Windstein [Old Windstein], built at the end of the 12th Century on a 350 metre-high sandstone rock: stairs, rooms, dungeons and wells, built from the rock. A 15-minute walk takes you to the Nouveau Windstein [New Windstein], which dates back to 1340. Its beautiful Gothic ogival windows have been preserved, as well as part of its fortifications.

Le Windstein stands out in the surrounding forest due to its amazing verticality.

Wasigenstein

Huge pink sandstone rocks suddenly appear by the side of Schlossberg, at a location of breathtaking beauty. These crown the ruins of the two 13th Century fortified châteaux, which are separated by a deep moat: to the East is the oldest and the highest, le Grand Wasigenstein and to the West le Petit. Legend has it that long before this date these rocks were witness to single combat between Walter, son of the king of the Wisigoths and Gunther, King of the Burgundians, who were competing for Attila's treasures, a fight which is recounted in the Waltharius, an epic poem of the 9th and 10th Centuries and part of the Niebelungen saga. The remains of the Wasigenstein châteaux include arched rooms with ogival windows, staircases carved out of the rock, as well as the cistern which is fed by numerous canals cut out of the sandstone.

This legendary château is mentioned in the Niebelungen saga.

Wasenbourg

Built in the 13th Century by the Bishop of Strasbourg, Jean de Lichtenberg and destroyed in the 17th Century by the troops of Louis XIV. A plaque commemorates the young Goethe passing through these places in 1771. You will see the remains of a delightful stately home with its nine beautiful ogival windows embellished with roses. From the summit, a very beautiful view of the Falkensteinbach valley and the surrounding area of Niederbronn.

Goethe too admired this delightful stately home.

5 Lichtenberg

Lichtenberg château is one of 35 ruins of châteaux that make up the North Vosges Nature Park and extends across an area of 1,220 km² between the Lower Rhine and the

from the fact that in times past, whenever a thunderstorm was approaching, one could see sparks flying on the keep's weathercock and on the halberds of the guards. This fort-

Second-hand market in the village's main street.

Moselle. Established in 1975, the park includes 108 communes and since 1998 has constituted the first cross-border biosphere in Europe to be recognised by the UNESCO.

Visible from afar, Lichtenberg Château stands on an imposing polygonal rock, the sides of which have been carved out with a pick. The name Lichtenberg originates

Lichtenberg Château
F-67340 Lichtenberg, Tel: 33(0)3 88 89 98 72
infos@chateaudelichtenberg.com
Guided tours throughout the year with advance booking

ress, a fief of the powerful Lichtenberg dynasty, of whom three bishops of Strasbourg bore the name, was built at the beginning of the 13th Century. Today, the visible vestiges mainly date back to the transformation undertaken by Daniel Specklin (architect of the city of Strasbourg) started from 1580 onwards.

In the 17th century, the château is captured by the troops of Louis XIV and is transformed into a fort.

The gothic style chapel, in which the Hanau-Lichtenberg family was buried, dates back to the end of the 14th century and contains an impressive Renaissance style mausoleum.

Le Lichtenberg, an exceptional site, serves as the backdrop for many theatrical performances.

6 Neuwiller-Les-Saverne

It was the transfer of the relics of Saint Adelphus (Bishop of Metz) to Neuwiller that gave the abbey, founded by the Benedictine monks in the 8th Century, its splendour by transforming it into a place of pilgrimage. On the main square stands l'église Saint Pierre et Saint Paul [St Peter and Paul Church], the two-tower façade of which dates from the 18th Century, like many beautiful canonical houses in the area. The whole of the church, however, dates back to the 12th and 13th Century, even to the 11th Century when it was the conventual two-floor former chapel which leans towards the sanctuary apse. The low Saint Catherine chapel in the Carolingian part makes up a crypt, whilst the high chapel, Saint Sebastian, displays beautiful carved cornices and has a collection of four tapestries dedicated to the life of Saint Adelphus and made in the abbey workshops in the 15th Century. The 14th Century chapter house is the sole remain of the old abbey.

The old Gothic-style collégiale St Adelphe [St Adelphus collegiate church] was built to house the Saint's relics and the pilgrims and is one of Alsace's first simultaneous churches, that is, shared between Protestants and Catholics after the Reformation. Today, it is entirely dedicated to the Protestant denomination.

The Saint Peter and Paul Church stands on this very beautiful square, which is lined with 18th Century buildings. Visit the remarkable tapestries representing the legendary life of St. Adelphus.

Information

Townhall. *7 rue Général Koenig, F-67730 Neuwiller-Les-Saverne*
Tel: 33(0)3 88 70 00 18
St Peter and Paul Abbey Church *Chapter Courtyard – Presbyterian.*
Tel: 33(0)3 88 70 00 51

7 La Petite Pierre

A little hiking paradise for gastronomic jaunts, as well as museums that range from the traditional (sceau alsacien [Museum of Alsatian Seal], springerle or carved with the château, of which the first owner Walter de Parva Petra, gave his name to the town from the year 1180. In Alsatian dialect it is known as "Lützelstein". The medi-

Aerial View of La Petite Pierre and its château

cake moulds) to the contemporary (an absolute must is the amazing Espace Mode de Cléone and its dignified exhibition of the world's greatest opera scenes). A visit to La Petite Pierre should commence aeval fortress was altered to a great extent in the 16th Century, then reinforced by Vauban. On entering, you will notice a long corridor built in 1831 and leading to the main buildings. Subsequently, you

---

Information

La Petite Pierre Region Tourist Office
2a, rue du Château, BP 16, F-67290 La Petite Pierre
Tel: 33(0)3 88 70 42 30 á Fax: 33(0)3 88 70 41 08
info@ot-paysdelapetitepierre.com – www.ot-paysdelapetitepierre.com
Musée du Sceau Alsacien [Museum of Alsatian Seal], *rue du Château –*
Chapelle St Louis. Tel: 33(0)3 88 70 48 65
La Petite Pierre Château, Parc naturel régional des Vosges du Nord
Tel: 33(0)3 88 01 49 59

View of the château from the ramparts, the seat of the North Vosges Regional Nature Park

can access the artillery platform and the powder magazine built on the foundations of a former tower. Then, take a tour of the ramparts which makes for a pleasant walk, enabling you to discover the galleries and their impressive subterranean cistern. In the château, 12 rooms house the headquarters of the Parc naturel régional des Vosges du Nord [North Vosges Regional Nature Park] which present the region and the heritage of this entity of more than one hundred communes. The church of La Petite Pierre continues to be used for both the Protestant and Catholic religion. It is decorated with beautiful frescos from the beginning of the 15th Century and features the tombs of several Elector princes of the Palatinate. In the town hall garden stands the house known as Maison des Païens [Pagan House], a Renaissance construction built on the foundations of a former Roman guards' tower. Finally, don't forget to pay a visit to the nearby Rock Houses carved in the Graufthal sandstone cliffs.

Rock Houses in Graufthal, inhabited right up until the 1950s

8 Sarre-Union

The gate to the North Vosges Regional Nature Park, Sarre-Union is also the capital of Alsace Bossue [Hunchbacked Alsace], the part of the region which is in the shape of a hooked nose, the outline of an

One of the architectural treasures.

enclave in Lorraine. Old land of the German Empire, Alsace Bossue was one of the last regions to be joined to France in 1789.

The Ville Neuve dates from the 18th Century church, of which the portal is decorated with a statue of Saint George on horseback and the inside with 18th Century woodcarvings. The town hall and numerous houses date from the same era. The Louis V design of the chapel of the old collège des Jésuites [Jesuit college] is also worth seeing. On the square, the greatly restored fountain is embellished with two 16th Century sandstone goats. The new town dates from the 18th Century as is shown by the two churches, the one

Guarded by two goats…

Lutheran and the other Calvinist, as well as some beautiful residences.

Regional Museum of Alsace Bossue – Former Jesuit College
Tel: 33(0)3 88 02 28 08
Townhall. Tel: 33(0)3 88 00 39 85

Information

9 Saint-Louis-Arzviller

Built in 1969, the inclined plane of Arzviller remains the only one in Europe with this kind of construction. It is a kind of boat lift which enables the barges on the Marne-Rhine canal to clear a 44.4 metre difference in height and thus avoid seventeen locks, which it would otherwise take a whole day to pass. The bin-truck, which moves transversely on the rails of a concrete ramp by means of a counterweight system and passes a barge from one reach to another in twenty minutes, is perfectly visible from the D 98 road.

However, it is just as interesting to take part in guided tours in a small motorboat. These last from one and a half to two hours and enable the visitors to descend the inclined plane and sail along the canal.

A view of the boat lift from a great height.

Tourist Association,
Plan incliné, F-57820 Saint-Louis, Tel: 33(0)3 87 25 30 69,
Fax: 33(0)3 87 25 41 82, www.plan-incline.com.fr

An aerial view of the overall inclined plane. It is the only transversal construction of this kind in Europe.

10 Saverne and the Haut-Barr Chateau

This town at the foot of a col with which it shares its name is 385 m at its highest point. Saverne was originally called Tres Tabernae – three taverns which were situated on the Roman road linking Strasbourg to Metz. When, in the 13th Century, the Bishop of Strasbourg was defeated by the bourgeoisie and lost his name of "Cardinal Collier" [Cardinal Necklace] due to the fact that he was the instigator of the famous affair of the Queen's necklace, which contributed to the downfall of Marie-Antoinette during the French Revolution. A reference to this chapter of history: the former tower known as de Cagliostro which

Boating in front of the Rohan Château which houses the town's museums.

power, he moved to Saverne, which subsequently became an Episcopal town. The current Rohan Château, a jewel of the town, was rebuilt by Salins de Montfort on the initiative of Cardinal Louis René de Rohan. This gentleman is known by the forms part of the town's oldest surrounding wall. During the 19th Century, the construction of the Marne-Rhine canal strengthened the town's role as a crossing point. Today, in the converted port, opposite the Rohan Château, on a canal

Saverne and Region Tourist Office, *37, Grand'Rue, F-67700 Saverne
Tel: 33(0)3 88 91 80 47 – Fax: 33(0)3 88 71 02 90
info@ot-saverne.fr; www.ot-saverne.fr*
Museum of the town of Saverne – Rohan Château
Tel: 33(0)3 88 91 06 28

Right in the town centre, one of the most highly visited locks by tourists, on the Marne-Rhine canal.

basin, one can still see numerous yachtsmen's boats, more than 7000 of which cast anchor each year.

For the pedestrian, a visit to Vieux Saverne [Old Saverne] commences with the Palais Rohan [Rohan Palace], the South façade of which stands on the place du Général-de-Gaulle, whilst the North side is extended by a formal garden which opens on to the canal basin. Every evening, the lights make this large pink sandstone building, which houses several museums, look even more majestic. The musée archéologique [Archaeological Museum] is situated in the cellars and both the musée historique [Historical

A very lively pedestrian centre with picturesque houses.

Overlooking the town of Saverne, the Haut-Barr Château was built in 1170 and

Museum] and the musée Louis Weiss [Louis Weiss Museum], dedicated to this convinced European and most senior member of the first European Parliament in 1979, can be found on the upper floors. With its cinema, video and documentary room, this museum is a veritable synopsis of the political and ideological history of the 20th Century. The left wing houses the youth hostel and a primary school. The opposite wing has housed the Rohan showroom since 1995, which, with its 500 seats, hosts around forty shows a year.

The rue Poincaré, on the other side of the place du Général -de-Gaulle

restored in 1583. Group guided tours are organised the whole year round.

leads to the former Recollects monastery and its 14th Century Gothic cloister. To the East of the château stands the old Oberhof or 17th Century château which houses the subprefecture. Another interesting church, which dates from the 15th Century, is l'Eglise Notre-Dame de la Nativité and its floral friezes on the ceiling have been restored. A large Romanesque red square porch tower marks the building from the outside. This parish church is a true museum with its pulpit dating from 1497, modelled on that of Strasbourg Cathedral which was created by Hans Hammer, as well as its 1482 jube, which was moved in the 18th

Century to be used as an organ loft at the entrance to the church. On returning to the Grand' Rue , several houses will attract your attention, notably the Renaissance-style town hall and maison Katz.

Before departing Saverne, you really should not miss the rose garden which, with 8,500 rose bushes and more than 500 varieties, offers the greatest variety of flowers in the East

Haut-Barr Château, built in the 12th Century, which keeps watch over the Alsace plain, earning it the nickname of Oeil d'Alsace [Eye of Alsace]. Built by Bishop Rodolphe de Rottweil, Bishop of Strasbourg, it extends across a high ridge made up of three 30-metre high rocks, two of which are linked by a foot bridge, which has been dubbed le pont du diable [the Devil's Bridge].

Aerial view of the Haut-Barr Château and its restaurant.

of France. This is situated 5 minutes from the town centre, on the route de Paris. You can follow this walk with a visit to the jardin botanique [botanical garden] and the Saut du Prince Charles [Prince Charles' Jump], situated halfway between Saverne and its col.

There are also round walks at the exit to Saverne, as 200 kilometres across mountains and forest have been marked out by the Vosges Club. Make it your priority to visit the

Some ten metres from the château, the famous Chappe telegraph pole served as a means of communication between Strasbourg and Paris from 1794 to 1852.

Katz Tavern · *80, Grand' Rue*
Tel: 33(0)3 88 71 16 56
And also Katz Villa on the route of the Saverne col, with hotel rooms.
Tel: 33(0)3 88 71 02 02
Clos de la Garenne · *88, route du Haut-Barr* · *Tel: 33(0)3 88 71 20 41*
Haut-Barr Château, *67700 Saverne*
Tel: 33(0)3 88 91 17 61

11 Dabo

From as far away as the village of la Hoube, at a height of 625 metres, the impressive silhouette of the Dabo rock stands out in the sky. It serves as a base for the Neoromanesque Chapelle Saint Léon [Chapel of St Leon] which replaced the château of the counts of Dabo and of which the 20m belvedere tower overlooks a large panorama. A panoramic table enables the visitor to locate the neighbouring summits of le Schneeberg, le Donon and le Grossmann. The statue of Léon IX reminds us of Bruno d'Eguisheim, the only Alsatian pope (from 1048 to 1054). The whole of Dabo, magnificent forest country, constitutes a very busy Summer resort.

Le Dabo, famous for the silhouette of its ship-shaped rock (664m high) on which stands the 19th Century Chapel of St Leon.

12 Marmoutier

Entirely in pink sandstone, the abbey façade of Marmoutier is one of Alsace's greatest successes of Century, it was expanded in the 18th Century in accordance with the principle of Carolingian

In the abbey church, the Silbermann organ dating from 1710, are used for numerous musical performances.

Romanesque architecture. It is best viewed at the end of the day, when the sun lights it up in all its glory. The abbey's origins date back to the 6th Century. Fallen into ruin, it was restored in 725 by Abbot Maur to whom it owes its name of Mauri Monasterium. Roughly treated during the peasant wars and from the 17th monuments - there are two octagonal towers surrounding a powerful square tower adorned with twin picture windows. In the centre, the three-arch porch is supported by beautiful cornice columns. Its rather sober decoration with pilaster strips is punctuated by several sculptures: heads, masks, six lions and a bear devouring a gateau. The

Marmoutier Region Tourist Office
1, rue du Général Leclerc. Tel: 33(0)3 88 71 46 84
tourisme.marmoutier@wanadoo.fr; www.marmoutier.net
Marmoutier Abbey Church, *8, place du Général de Gaulle*
Museum of Popular Art and Tradition, *6, rue du Général Leclerc.*
Tel: 33(0)3 88 71 46 84

13th and 14th Century nave is Gothic, whilst the choir and apse date from the 18th Century. Inside, you can view the decoration of the cornices, the 16th Century pulpit, the Silbermann organs from 1709 and the Louis XV stalls of the choir. Excavations have been carried out at the church which is bordered by 17th and 18th Century canonical houses. It is well worth a visit to the Musée des Arts et Traditions Populaires [Museum of Popular Art and Tradition], which is situated in a beautiful 16th Century half-timbered house.

On its completely renovated esplanade stands the impressive Romanesque façade of the abbey church, entirely made of pink sandstone.

13 Haguenau

The town was built bit by bit around one of the numerous châteaux of Friedrich the One-Eyed at the beginning of the 12th Century. It was said of him that he always dragged a fortified château with the tail of his horse. Friedrich Barbarossa transformed this into a palace where his grandson, Emperor Friedrich II, the last of the Hohenstaufen line, held a magnificent court. There no longer remains anything of this splendour which was destroyed by Louvois in the 18th Century in order to break down the resistance of this town which was resisting the King

The Alsatian Museum, housed by the former mediaeval chancery reveals the traditions of yesteryear.

Information

Haguenau Tourist Office, Place de la Gare, F-67500 Haguenau
Tel: 33(0)3 88 93 70 00 – Fax: 33(0)3 88 93 69 89
tourisme@ville-haguenau.fr; www.ville-haguenau.fr
Alsatian Museum, 1, place Joseph Thierry. Tel: 33(0)3 88 73 30 41
Musée Historique [Museum of History], 9, rue du Maréchal Foch. Tel: 33(0)3 88 93 79 22, *Nautiland Leisure and bathing activity.* Tel. 33(0)3 88 90 56 56
www.nautiland.net

Three towers of former fortifications mark the urban countryside.

Fountains and flowerbeds make up the town's charm.

of France. Of the former fortifications with no less than 54 towers, there remain only three: la Tour des Chevaliers [Knights' Tower], la Tour des Pêcheurs [Fishermen's Tower], which spans the Moser River, and la Porte de Wissembourg [Wissembourg Gate]. There remain just two of the 29 churches: Saint Georges started in the 12th and completed in the 15th Century. Two Romanesque towers surround the central steeple where two of the oldest bells in Alsace sound their chimes. (1268). Inside the Church a very beautiful flamboyant Gothic-style tabernacle (1523), 14m in height, a pulpit and a 16th Century altarpiece. In front of the Church, the 18th Century fountain originates from the former Neubourg Abbey. Founded by Emperor Barbarossa in

the 12th Century, then given to the Premonstratensians, l'église Saint-Nicolas [Church of Saint Nicholas] was entirely reconstructed in the 14th Century. The two statues which adorn the portal represent Saint Nicholas and Saint Norbert. The inside of the Church features exceptional 18th Century wainscotting, which is also from Neubourg Abbey. There is also a 16th Century Holy Sepulchre and a pietà. At the entrance to the choir stand four wooden statues representing the Fathers of the Church: Augustine, Ambrose, Gregory and Jerome.

The main street and the parade ground are bordered by 18th Century houses. Haguenau has two remarkable museums: Alsatian Museum with its costumes and furniture, as well as Museum of Art

Housed in an impressive Neo-Renaissance building, the Museum of History features some beautiful collections.

A very contemporary setting for the archaeological collections.

and History, which includes a rare collection of silver gilt tumblers and books printed in Haguenau between 1484 and 1550. Close by the museum stands the secondary school chapel, which has preserved its beautiful 15th Century frescos. Finally,Fleckenstein hotel (1480) and the Dislach mill with its paddle wheel also constitute part of

this tourist round walk in this town which is signposted at the entrance by a flower sundial.

Sessenheim

It is here that one remembers the frantic rides of Goethe, across forests and mountains, who came here to meet Frédérique Brion, the pastor's daughter with whom he was madly in love. Even today, the whole of Sessenheim is devoted to the worship of the great poet. A memorial is dedicated to him, as well as the musée à l'Auberge du Boeuf [Ox Inn Museum]. If you walk a little further, you will reach chêne de Frédérique or Frédérique's Oak ...

The "Au Boeuf" restaurant houses a museum passionately devoted to the memory of Goethe.

14 Soufflenheim and Betschdorf

These villages are two historic centres of Alsatian pottery. In Soufflenheim, where the existence of potters since the 12th Century has been attested, craftsmen make glazed earthenware pottery which is intended for cooking food, for example, the moules à kougelhopf [kugelhopf – a kind of cake - moulds] or the pots à baeckeoffe. Each item is coated both inside and out by a white-cream, yellow, green or blue engobe. On top of this, decorations are applied by using barrolets, kinds of coloured reservoirs finished off with a goose quill. After firing, the polychrome drawings – flowers, birds, geometric shapes – reveal their true brilliance. It was in the 18th Century that potters from Germany introduced the Rhenish technique of salt stoneware to Betschdorf. It is used for making food utensils for storing food products, eggs, sauerkraut, turnips or wine pitchers or brandy casks and is easily recognisable by its grey colour enhanced with blue cobalt drawings. Salt stoneware stands out due to its firing method which requires 50 hours, during which several quintals of salt are thrown into the kiln, which is what gives the pottery its special appearance. Best of all is a visit to one of the numerous workshops which line the streets of these villages and whose doors are wide open to visitors. The musée de la poterie [pottery museum], located in one of these beautiful 18th Century half-timbered houses, for which Betschdorf is so renowned, is also well worth a visit. It presents the evolution of the region's pottery from the Neolithic age up until the present day, as well as a reconstruction of a workshop.

Betschdorf, at the workshop of LOÏS the potter.

Soufflenheim Tourist Office
20 b, Grand'Rue, F-67620 Soufflenheim
Tel: 33(0)3 88 86 74 90 – Fax: 33(0)3 88 86 60 69
infos@ot-soufflenheim.fr; www.ot-soufflenheim.fr
Pottery Museum in Betschdorf. *Tel: 33(0)3 88 54 48 07*

Many pottery workshops are open to the public the whole year round.

Beautiful example of coloured Soufflenheim pottery: the terrines indispensable for making the famous baeckeoffe.

Drawings meticulously done by hand before being fired in the salt kiln.

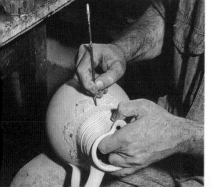

15 Hunspach and Seebach

These two villages are among the best preserved in Alsace and women are frequently seen in regional dress, which is one of the most beautiful in Alsace and worn on which is predominantly Protestant with large farm buildings. The lower part is predominantly Catholic, whilst the 18th Century town hall is situated in the middle.

Aerial view of the procession during the "Streisselhochzeit" in July in Seebach.

Sundays or on special occasions.

The product of the union of Oberseebach [Upper Seebach] and Niederseebach [Lower Seebach], Seebach is part of the villages – a one-street village the upper part of Notice the fortified Catholic church and its keep just above. An ancient lime tree stands on the town square of Protestant Hunspach. Its plantation, as a tree of liberty, dates back to 1789. The settlement is grouped

Hunspach Tourist Office, *3, Rte de Hoffen, F-67250 Hunspach.*
Tel.: 33(0)3 88 80 59 39 – Fax: 33(0)3 88 80 41 46
Schoenenbourg Fort, *maison-ungerer@wanadoo.fr;*
www.maison-ungerer.com, www.lignemaginot.com

Many spectators attentively follow the procession in the idyllic setting of the village.

around the courtyards of the farm which opens on to the street, the roofs are covered with biberschwanz or flat tiles in the shape of a beaver's tale, and the windows, which often have bulging panes, as was the fashion during the Baroque period, enabling the inhabitants to look out on to the street without being seen, are generally protected from bad weather by small awnings. Note also: The tiered fountains.

Discover Hunspach, one of the prettiest towns in France and the fortress Schöneburg, the most impressive building of the Maginot-Line of Alsace.

Typical national costumes in Hunspach, the northern Alsace.

45

16 Strasbourg

Seat of the Council of Europe, of the European Court of Human Rights and meeting place for the European Parliament, with its urban community, Strasbourg has a of total of 28 communes and 450 000 inhabitants. Its origins date back to the Romans who chose this site for a military camp on the Rhine, which they named

Argentoratum. In the 7th Century, destroyed by barbarian invasions, the agglomeration was revived under the name of Strateburgum, a city at the Crossroads of Europe.

It prospered in the Middle Ages during the Holy Roman German Empire and experienced a golden age during the Renaissance, when it became one of the cradles of printing. In 1681, it was reattached to the Kingdom of France. Within its walls was born the French national anthem, "The Marseillaise". After the last war in 1949, it became the seat of the Council of Europe.

Aerial view of Strasbourg with the European institutions in the foreground.

◄ In front of the Cathedral, always a very lively square.

The Cathedral is a departure point for the tour of the town for visitors. The building stands on a large paved square just as in the Middle Ages. It rests on the foundations of an old Rhenish basilica, built in 1015 by Bishop Wernher of the Hapsburg family. Destroyed by fire, it was replaced by a new cathedral. Almost three centuries elapsed, from the foundations begun in 1176 to the spire which wasn't completed until 1439. Up until the 19th Century, Strasbourg's 142-metre-high Notre-Dame Cathedral was the highest Christian building. Part of the crypt and the apse are remains of the old Wernherian basilica. Around 1225, the arrival of a group from Chartres revolutionised the course of its construction. A project manager whose name introduced the local artisans to the splendours of Gothic art. He left behind various works of art, such as the Pillar of Angels and statues of the Church and of the Synagogue (Southern transept). Some fifty years later, construction began on the main façade, which remains the most ornate. The tympana of its three portals are dedicated to the life of Christ and to the Last Judgement. The famous group of the Tempter, surrounded by the Foolish Virgins decorates the right portal and was used as the model for the cathedrals of Freiburg and Basel. On the left portal, the Virtues pierce the Vices with their lance. An astonishingly light double gable surmounts the portals. A marvellous rose blooms in a fine fretwork stone frame and is believed to have been created by Erwin de Steinbach, project manager of the Cathedral from 1284 to 1318. On top of this two towers linked by the belfry, which was constructed as late as the end of

Information

Strasbourg and Region Tourist Office
17, Place de la Cathédrale, Tel: 33(0)3 88 52 28 28,
Fax: 33(0)3 88 52 28 29, info@otstrasbourg.fr; www.otstrasbourg.fr
Reception Office in the Cathedral, Reception Office in the Station
Guided tours of the city on bateau-mouche Batorama, 15, rue de
Nantes, F-67100 Strasbourg, Tel. 33(0)3 88 84 13 13, Fax: 33(0)3 88 84 33 13
info@batorama.fr; www.batorama.fr
Museums:
**Rohan Palace (Museum of Decorative Arts, Museum of Fine Arts,
Archaeological Museum)**, 2, Place du Château, Tel: 33(0)3 88 52 50 00
Musée de l'Oeuvre Notre-Dame, 3, Place du Château, Tel: 33(0)3 88 52 50 00
Alsatian Museum, 23 Quai Saint-Nicolas, Tel: 33(0)3 88 52 50 00
Museum of Contemporary and Modern Art, 1, Place Hans Jean Arp
Tel: 33(0)3 88 23 31 31
History Museum, 2, rue du Vieux-Marché-aux-Poissons, Tel: 33(0)3 88 52 50 90
Zoology Museum, 29, Boulevard de le Victoire, Tel: 33(0)3 90 24 04 83
Tomi Ungerer Museum, Centre International de l'Illustration, Villa Grenier,
2, Avenue de la Marseillaise, Tel: 33(0)3 69 06 37 27
Visits to the Council of Europe. Tel: 33(0)3 88 41 20 29.
Visits to the European Parliament, on for groups and on prior written request to:
Antenna du Parlement européen (European Parliament Branch), Allée des
Printemps – B.P. 1024 F-67070 Strasbourg Cedex
Bas-Rhin Tourism Development Agency, Tel: 33(0)3 88 15 45 80,
Fax: 33(0)3 88 75 67 64, adt@tourisme67.com; www.tourisme67.com

Underneath the Romanesque cupola, the choir which has been remodelled several times over.

the 14th Century, make up the platform. From this height, after having climbed some three hundred and twenty-six stairs, you can enjoy a beautiful panorama of the town and its surroundings. On the platform stands the octagonal tower, surmounted by a fretwork spire by Jean Hulz of Cologne. On the South side of the Cathedral, the beautiful portal of the Clock, the oldest portal, is flanked by copies of statues of the Church and the Synagogue, the originals of which, like many of the Cathedral's other statues, are kept in the Musée de l'Oeuvre Notre-Dame. The tympanum of the right-hand door depicts the Crowning of the Virgin. The North side portal is dedicated to Saint Lawrence, the martyr of whom – a modern copy – is depicted above the door, surmounted by a marvellous flamboyant Gothic-style baldachin. The piers are adorned with the Magi from the end of the 15th Century. Inside, the nave, built in two separate phases between 1240 and 1275, is fascinating due to the harmony of its proportions. It has preserved the majority of its original stained-glass windows, the oldest of which date back to the 13th Century and are situated in the lower North side and depict the sovereigns of the Holy Roman German Empire. In the 14th Century, the Chapel of St Catherine was added to the nave, with its very special stained-glass windows from the same era. The Chapel of Saint Lawrence, the stained-glass windows of which originate from the old Dominican Church, was added during the same period. The Northern transept features the Mount of Olives from 1498 and the flamboyant Gothic-style baptismal fonts dating from 1453. It is here that you can find the most amazing stained-glass windows in the whole of the building. Originating from the former Wernherian basilica, these represent the two Saint Johns, the Baptist and the Evangelist, as well as a Pieta and a Judgement of Solomon with a profusion of bright green.

At the end of the transept, the Chapel of Saint John the Baptist houses the 14th Century tomb of Bishop Conrad of Lichtenberg, as well as an epitaph of Nicolas Gerhard de Leyde (1464) representing a canon in prayer in front of a Virgin with Child.

The pulpit by Hans Hammer is a superb example of flamboyant Gothic style architecture. The organ

The Pillar of the Angel and the famous astronomical clock with its automatons.

chest, decorated with peculiar characters, is also from the end of the Middle Ages. According to a custom which survived up until the Reformation, its articulate mannequins acted as mouthpieces for hidden speakers and never missed a chance to denounce the abuse of the Church during the service on Easter Sunday.

In the Southern transept, other automatons which are still in operation animate the Astronomical Clock. This clock is a legacy of the Reformation. It was constructed around 1547 by a team of Swiss clockmakers. Out of use from the Revolution, it was repaired by Jean-Baptiste Schwilgué who enhanced it with a Copernican planetary and an Ecclesiastical computation. The movement of all the characters of this clock – and notably the cock crow – symbolises the denial of the apostle Peter and is thus the Cathedral's major attraction every day at 12.30 p.m. In front of the clock stands the marvellous Pillar of Angels, which in fact represents the Last Judgement.

You shouldn't leave the place de la Cathédrale without taking a look at the Maison Kammerzell, the most beautiful half-timbered house in Strasbourg. It catches your imagination due to its incredible profusion of sculpted décor. It is a veritable book containing all the themes dear to the Renaissance: the heroes of the Bible and of

In the shadow of the Cathedral, Strasbourg's most beautiful half-timbered house: maison Kammerzell.

Antiquity, the ten ages of life and the five senses. The corner post is decorated with three magisterial sculptures: Faith, Hope and Charity. Inside, under the Gothic vaults of the ground floor, large painted frescoes from the 14th Century, created by Léo Schnug, enhance the building's cosy atmosphere.

Rue Mercière features several very beautiful 16th and 17th Century houses, of which number 8 boasts a splendid balcony, added in the 18th Century.

On place de Gutenberg stands the Chamber of Commerce building, which was formerly the town hall, built in the 16th Century. The statue of Gutenberg by David d'Angers (1840) occupies the centre of the square. On Rue de l'Epine is a succession of special hotels from the 17 and 18th Centuries, built by rich merchants, who were anxious to live in close proximity to the Ancienne Douane [Former Customs Office], the town's economic centre in the Middle Ages. Hôtel Zorn at number 9 and the richly decorated portal of number 3 are two buildings well worth a visit.

Rue de la Douane, on the right, runs into quai Saint Thomas where the former university buildings, built in the 18th Century, house the Protestant Seminary and the Executive Board of the Augsburg Confession. Exceptionally beautiful 18th Century hotels, the façades of which are punctuated by elegant ironwork.

Rue Saint Thomas, to the right,

runs into the square of the same name, where the Church stands, which is also one of the most important Lutheran parish churches. Built between the 12th and 14th Centuries, the église Saint Thomas [Church of Saint Thomas] is a typical example of the five-nave hall church, which is popular in the Rhineland and the Nether-

The mausoleum of Marshal de Saxe, sculpted by Pigalle

lands. The inside houses a veritable museum of funerary monuments. The most famous one is incontestably the mausoleum of Marshal de Saxe, project manager of the 18th Century statuary by the sculptor Pigalle. In a little Chapel is the 12th Century tomb of Bishop Adeloch. In the Southern transept is a beautiful 13th Century tympanum, which depicts the disbelief of Saint Thomas. It is from here that one enters Petite

On Place Benjamin Zix, painters just as at Montmartre. Maison des Tanneurs [Tanners' House], former seat of this guild.

France [Little France], the most evocative district of old Strasbourg, which extends from the Church of Saint Thomas to the Ponts Couverts [Covered Bridges]. Formerly the district of fishermen, millers and tanners, it owes its name to a hospital specialising in the treatment of syphilis, or "French illness", brought from Italy by the troops of François I. The streets of Petite France, rue des Dentelles [Lace Street], rue du Bain-aux-Plantes [Herbal Bath Street], display a succession of half-timbered houses with spacious inside courtyards, large sloping roofs that open on to lofts, the majority of which are low constructions to allow the tanners to dry their skins. You shouldn't miss the Rathsamhausen Hotel, an aristocratic building inspired by the Renaissance, hidden amongst artisan houses, the most typical of which is undoubtedly the Maison

Tourist motorboats cross la Petite France both night and day.

des Tanneurs [Tanners' House] with its extremely flowery wooden galleries. Opposite stands le Lohkäs, the name of which is reminiscent of the tannin used to dry skins. After use this material was placed in a mould and dried and then recycled as a fuel. Let us leave this little street in order to cross the rotating bridge, a metallic bridge from the last Century which folds up to allow the passage of tourist boats sailing on the Ill.

This stage of our journey is followed by passing under the vaulted porch to cross the public garden of Petite France, a little delta between two arms of the Ill, and arrive at the Ponts Couverts.

Ponts Couverts (or "Bun Gewehr", depending on the Strasbourg pronunciation) are 13th Century remains of the important belt of fortifications which surrounded the town. Three large square towers overlook the bridges, covered over with roofs up until the 18th Century, lending them a certain resemblance to Ponte Vechio in Florence.

Opposite stands the Vauban Dam. After Strasbourg was reattached to France, a new belt of fortifications was constructed by Vauban, of which the dam is a part. The lowering of its iron sluice gates enables the entire South front of the town to be flooded in case of invasion.

These days, the Vauban Dam has been transformed into a panoramic terrace, enabling one to take in an overall view of Strasbourg with a single glance. It is here that the Ill,

a Rhine tributary, divides into five canals. To the South, three of these flow in the direction of the quartier des Moulins [Mills Quarter], where they turn the paddles. In the centre, the ship canal is still used even today. To the North flows the canal du Faux Rempart [Canal of the False Rampart], which is so-named due to the crenellated wall which used to separate the waterway. At the entrance to this canal stands the Commanderie St Jean and its steeple, which, up until the 16th Century provided accommodation for the Knights of St John of Jerusalem and today welcomes the pupils of the Ecole National d'Administration (ENA) [National School of Management]. The oldest part of the building is decorated with a trompe-l'œil façade. This can be reached by crossing the ground floor from the Vauban Dam, which has been converted into a pedestrian passage linking Pont Couverts to Place des Anciens Abattoirs [Old Abattoirs Square]. It is here that you will find Strasbourg's Museum of Modern and Contemporary Art.

We then retrace our steps in the direction of the town centre, following the quays of the Ill with their very picturesque houses, such as those which make up the Musée Alsacien [Alsatian Museum] – numbers 23, 24 and 25 of quai Saint Nicolas. Scattered along the opposite bank are the Corbeau bridge, the Old Mediaeval Customs Office and the old Renaissance butchers and home of the Historical Museum which is currently undergoing restoration. By following the promenade on the quai des Bateliers [Boatmens' Quay], you will come out opposite Palais Rohan.

In front of the building is a spacious terrace, which bore witness to sumptuous festivities. From 1704 to the Revolution, the Rohan family were to monopolise Strasbourg's Episcopal seat. The first of this line, Armand Gaston de Rohan Soubise, appealed to the King's architect, Robert de Cotte, to draw up the plans for the Palace, which was created by Joseph Massol. Nothing was too beautiful for the natural son of Louis XIV, whose motto was "Rois ne puis, Prince ne daigne, Rohan suis" ["King, I cannot be, Prince I deign not to be, Rohan am I"]. The building work, begun in 1730, wasn't completed until ten years later during which a succession of artists and artisans came from the whole of Europe. When the château was finished, King Louis XV was the first visitor to stay in the princely apartments, the designs of which were based on Versailles.

Reinforced remains of mediaeval fortifications of the town, a 16th Century bastion

Today, the Rohan Palace houses several museums. The Decorative Arts Museum takes the visitor right back to the 18th Century. It is dedicated to the famous earthenware pieces of Hannong manufacture. Its delicately coloured plates and its incredible trompe-l'œil pieces are worth the trip. The Musée des Beaux-Arts [Fine Arts Museum], which specialises in Italian and Flemish painting, exhibits works of art by Giotto, Raphael, Véronèse, Lucas de Leyde, Jacob von Ruysdäel and Peter de Hoog. However, other countries are also represented, in particular Spain with a remarkable "Mater Dolorosa" by Greco and portraits by Goya. One of the Museum's most impressive exhibits is "La Belle Strasbourgeoise" [The Beautiful Strasbourg Lady], painted in 1703 by Nicolas de Largillière.

The Musée Archéologique [Archaeological Museum] is situated in the basement and is the oldest museum in Strasbourg. It is also the newest as it was entirely restored in order to present its rich collections in the most attractive

in the foreground.

Rue du Maroquin on a hot Summer night with its many terraces.

way possible and in a manner in keeping with the contemporary museographical presentation. From paleography to the Merovingian era, Alsace's entire past is exhibited here. You can return to the Cathedral from the Rohan Palace by passing in front of the beautiful semi-detached buildings of the Musée de l'Oeuvre Notre Dame which has been dedicated to Alsatian art since its beginnings back in the 17th Century and exhibits original statues of the Cathedral.

A l'Abattoir, 16, Place Abattoir. Tel: 44(0)3 88 26 29 60
  Au Crocodile (gastronomic), 10, rue de Loutre. Tel: 33(0)3 88 32 13 02
Le Fossile, Place des Orphelins. Tel: 33(0)3 88 36 39 76
Maison Kammerzell, 16, Place de la Cathédrale. Tel: 33(0)3 88 32 42 14
Maison des Tanneurs, 42, rue du Bain-aux-Plantes. Tel: 33(0)3 88 32 79 70
Lohkäs, rue du Bain-aux-Plantes. Tel: 33(0)3 88 32 05 26
La Table Thaïlandaise Chan Chira, rue des Moulins. Tel: 33(0)3 88 32 68 34
Umami, gastronomic, 8, rue des Dentelles, Tel: 33(0)3 88 32 80 53
Hôtel Cathédrale, 12, Place de la Cathédrale. Tel: 33(0)3 88 22 12 12

La Wantzenau, Offendorf village, Les écluses de Gambsheim

To the north of Strasbourg, La Wantzenau is an old fishing village with numerous half-timbered houses. Small flat-bottomed boats dot the River Ill as it winds its way through the Rhenish forest. A halt in this countryside is both bucolic due to its walks and gastronomic due to its abundance of good restaurants.

La Wantzenau townhall, F-67610. Tel: 33(0)3 88 59 22 59

By the side of the Ill, magical and unforgettable moments.

The large flat fishing boats are still used in everyday life as well as at festivals.

Information

Offendorf, *Navigation and Inland Waterways Museum, Cabro houseboat.*
Tel: 33(0)3 88 96 43 79 (Guided visits)
Nautic-Port, *4, Rte du Port, F-67850 Offendorf. Tel: 33(0)3 88 96 43 79*
contact@nautic-port.fr, **Tourist Office, Les écluses de Gambsheim.**
F-6776°0 Gambsheim, Tel: 33(0)3 88 96 44 08, Fax: 33(0)3 88 59 73 11
One of the three major inland waterway nagivation locks of Europ.To visit: the Fish pass.

17 Molsheim

To enter the town centre one has to pass beneath the porte des Forgerons or Blacksmiths' Gate (1412). A little further on, on the Place de l'Hôtel de ville, a fountain decorated with a lion bearing the town's coat of arms stands in front of la Metzig, the former seat of the butchers' guild. This beautiful Renaissance building is very striking due to its balcony, its double staircase and its automated clock. The collégiale Saint-Georges [St George Collegiate Church] or Jesuit Church was built between the years of 1614 and 1618. The style is a combination of Gothic and Renaissance. It is reminiscent of the fact that Molsheim was one of the bastions of the 17th Century Counter-Reformation. Close to

A remarkable late Gothic-style church: the Church of the Jesuits.

Molsheim-Mutzig Region Tourist Office
19, place de l'Hôtel de Ville, F-67120 Molsheim
Tel: 33(0)3 88 38 11 61 – Fax: 33(0)3 88 49 80 40
infos@ot-lolsheim-mutzig.com
Charterhouse and Bugatti Foundation Museum
4, Cour des Chartreux, F-67120 Molsheim, Tel: 33(0)3 88 49 59 38
www.chartreuse-molsheim.info
Mutzig Fortress. *Tel: 33(0)6 08 84 17 42, info@fort.mutzig.eu*
Mutzig Regional Weapon Museum, *Place Jacques Coulaux, F-67190 Mutzig*
Tel: 33(0)3 88 38 31 98

The completely redeveloped town hall square

In a bosky bower, the Dompeter steeple, a moving testimony of the beginnings of Romanesque art.

Molsheim, the Bugatti factory has been given a new lease of life and is now once again manufacturing the famous cars of this brand.

Mutzig

A small town which was fortified in times past. There remains a gate surmounted by a square tower decorated with a mural painting of St Maurice. Rebuilt in the 17th Century, the château was a 19th Century base for weapons manufacture, where Chassepot, born in 1833 in Mutzig, perfected a rifle which was to become his namesake. A visit to the fortress or Kaiser Wilhelm II citadel, and in particular its knife collection, is highly recommended.

61

18 Marlenheim

A small town reputed for its Steinklotz Grand Cru wine and its Marlenheim red wine. The Merovingian kings set up one of their "villas" here. The Baroque church has preserved a Romanesque lintel from the end of the 11th Century, depicting Christ presenting the keys to Saint-Peter and the Gospels to Saint-Paul. In the town centre, the Ancienne Douane is reminiscent of Marlenheim's commercial vocation and today marks the beginning of the Route des Vins, which ends about one hundred and twenty kilometres further on, in Thann. Marlenheim is also situated on the couronne d'or, a reference to the crown of the Merovingian kings, which constitutes one of the vineyard routes of the lower Rhine and groups together twenty-one wine-growing communes around Strasbourg.

Le Cerf · 30, rue du Général-de-Gaulle · Tel: 33(0)3 88 87 73 73 Also hotel rooms

In the heart of the vineyard, a small chapel and its Way of the Cross are among the hidden treasures of Marlenheim.

Tourist Office
*Place du Kaufhus. Tel – Fax: 33(0)3 88 87 75 80
info@tourisme-marlenheim.fr; www.tourisme-marlenheim.fr*

One of those neat and charming villages for which Alsace is reputed and which marks the beginning of the vineyard route.

Everywhere there → are wine cellars to be visited.

Overall view of the ↓ town hall.

19 Rosheim

Fortified for the first time in the 13th Century, Rosheim was refortified in the 15th Century. A first circular surrounding wall is accompanied by a second and longer wall, which encloses the houses lining the road. Of these city walls, three fortified gates remain of which one, the porte des Lions , overlooks the vineyard. St Peter and Paul is a marvellous Romanesque Church built by the Hohenstaufen dynasty between 1132 and 1190. A Gothic style steeple surmounts the transept crossing. The external decorations are striking, in particular the Southern side portal, the decoration of the apse of which the central window is framed by the symbols of the four Evangelists and in the corners of the

Aerial view of Rosheim with the Saint Peter and Paul Church in the centre, a masterpiece of Romanesque art.

Tourist Office
94, rue du Gl de Gaulle, F-67560 Rosheim
Tel: 33(0)3 88 50 75 38
accueil@rosheim.com

Information

main façade, four lions devouring a man. The very sober inside is softened by the alternation of square pillars and columns with sculpted cornices. The sacristy from the beginning of the 12th Century was built on top of the choir of a former church.

On the main square stands the 18th Century town hall, the Zittgloeckelturm or clock tower and a very beautiful Renaissance well.

The 12th Century maison païenne or pagan house, the oldest residential building in Alsace, is situated in the upper part of town. The Saint-Etienne church, built by the architect of the Saverne Château, dates back to the 17th Century, whilst having preserved its 13th Century steeple.

Hostellerie du Rosenmeer –
(Gastronomic) 45, avenue de la
Gare · Tel: 33(0)3 88 50 43 29
La Petite Auberge 41, rue du Général
de Gaulle · Tel: 33(0)3 88 50 40 60

Pass beneath the mediaeval gates, truly enchanting.

A glimpse of Saint Peter and Paul overlooking Rosheim's half-timbered houses.

65

Le Grand Donon (1009m) is one of the oldest sites of the Celtic then Gallo-Roman religion. Numerous archaeological remains have been found on this ground. These include: the foundations of several temples where the Celts practiced the cult to the stag-headed god, Cernunnos and Gallo-Roman Mercury. At the very top of the summit a Neohellenistic church which was built in the 19th Century during the reign of Napoleon III. Numerous graffitos and inscriptions surround this. A stone tablet certifies that Victor Hugo was conceived here. In the middle of the footpath that leads to this, you can see a sculpture inspired by a Gallo-Roman bas relief that was discovered on the summit and represents Jupiter and the serpent-footed monster. However, the majority of the remains are gathered in the Epinal and Strasbourg museums. A cemetery from the Great War is situated close by, as this place, which is peppered with blockhouses and gun carriages, connected by underground galleries – was witness to a great number of combats.

One of the Vosges' great mythical places: the summit of the Donon and its temple.

21 Obernai

Traditionally the birthplace of Saint Odilia as we are reminded by the ornate fountain decorated with her statue which stands in the centre of the marketplace. This square is surrounded by the most beautiful monuments of this town which has managed to preserve its old mediaeval and Renaissance setting. Dating from 1462, the town hall has been renovated several times and features a bay window and a Gothic balcony

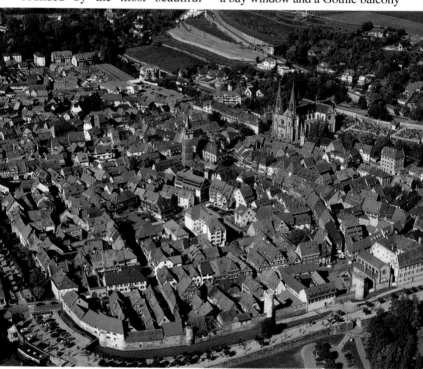

Obernai seen from the air in the soft Autumn light which highlights its mediaeval wall.

Tourist Office, Place du Beffroi, F-67210 Obernai
Tel: 33(0)3 88 95 00 37 – Fax: 33(0)3 88 49 90 84
visites@obernai.fr; www.obernai.fr
Free guided tours during summer, contact the Tourist Office.

from 1604. The conference room is situated in the former court room with its richly sculpted wainscotting. The 1609 frescoes represent the Ten Commandments. The Kappelturm or belfry, 59.60 meters in height, is the adjacent building. As its name suggests, this was the bell tower of a mediaeval chapel which today no longer exists. Opposite stands the 16th Century Ancienne Boucherie, used as an abattoir and then a wheat market and today a restaurant. It is easily recognisable by its high roof and sharp gable.

In front of the De la Cloche hotel where the works of Charles Spindler, an Alsatian artist from the beginning of the 20th Century, are exhibited, stands the most beautiful well in Alsace. Dating from 1579, it is fitted with three wheels and six buckets. An inscription evokes the meeting of Jesus and the Samaritan at Jacob's well. The church from the end of the 19th Century boasts several beautiful 15th Century stained-glass windows, as well as a 1504 altar with an altarpiece representing Christ's burial and resurrection. In the church's adjoining cemetery, there is a Mount of Olives dating from 1517 as well as a pretty chapel

Obernai: The perfect setting for all traditional Alsatian festivals.

◄ The most beautiful well in Alsace with its six buckets.

Right out of an album by ► de Hansi…

The market place and its Wheat Hall overflowing with festive spirit.

Summery atmosphere, Obernai in the sun.

which it is worth visiting.

However, Obernai's true charm lies in the walk down its alleyways with their picturesque names and where the houses line the streets in a higgle-depiggledy fashion. Everywhere, amazing details that should not be passed by without a closer look: sculptured windows, portals topped with guild emblems. The most frequently recurring motif remains that of the pruning knife with a bunch of grapes and a vinestock. The most interesting houses are the maison Fastinger and its courtyard, 68, rue du Général-Gouraud and the maison Strohn, 8, rue des Pèlerins. The Obernai ramparts enable you to have a pleasant walk around the town. The moats are today planted with vines, flowers and fruit trees, whilst the view inside the houses embedded in the ramparts is concealed by narrow loopholes.

70

Les Remparts Restaurant
3, rue du Marché
Tel: 33(0)3 88 95 15 52
La Halle aux Blés [Wheat Hall]
Place du Marché · Tel: 33(0)3 88 95 56 09
La Dîme
5, rue des Pèlerins · Tel: 33(0)3 88 95 54 02
La Fourchette des Ducs - gastronomique
6, rue de la Gare · tél: 33(0)3 88483338
Le Parc – (Gastronomic) · 169, route
d'Ottrott · Tel: 33(0)3 88 95 50 08 · Hotel-restaurant, but also wine tavern from midday

Patron saint of Alsace, Saint Odilia watches over Obernai.

Take a walk in Obernai: a dream.

The „holy mountain" of Alsace is the most popular pilgrimage and is located on a 763 m-high promontory. It is surrounded by a 10,5 km wall made up of course sandstone blocks that are joined together using wooden tenons. This Mur Païen [Pagan Wall] actually dates

Mont-Sainte-Odile, F-67530 Ottrott
Tel: 33(0)3 88 95 80 53 – Fax: 33(0)3 88 95 82 96
info@mont-sainte-odile.com; www.mont-sainte-odile.com
Open from 8:00 am to 9:30 pm the whole year round.

Information

back to the era of Etichon, Duke of Alsace, who founded this convent in the 7th Century on the site of a Merovingian fortress, known as "Hohenbourg" and whose daughter, Odilia, was the first abbess. Initially rejected by her father as she was born blind, Odilia was brought up in

Alsace's most popular pilgrimage: Mont Sainte Odile atop its rocky spur. Overall view of the convent and of the church.

Bourgogne and recovered her sight when she was baptised. She was credited with numerous miracles during her lifetime, namely of having made a spring gush forth to cure the blind. After her death, around the year 720, her burial place became an object of worship. In the older parts of the convent, the sarcophagus of the Chapel of Saint John the Baptist continues to welcome a large number of visitors. Like the conventual church, the chapelle Sainte Croix [the Chapel of the Holy Cross] and the exterior chapels, this chapel has some of the attributes of a reconstruction phase of the convent during the 12th Century, but the whole of the building has experienced a great deal of modifications since this time. You will be inevitably enchanted by the spirit of this place as soon as you have crossed the large porch which leads to the courtyards planted with lime trees, to the church and to the salle des pèlerins [pilgrims' room]. This feeling will intensify once you catch sight of the panoramic view which unfurls from the terraces surrounding the church which is overlooked by the statue of the saint. The two terrace chapels are each decorated with modern mosaics. Inside the chapelle des Larmes [Chapel of Tears], a long-established tradition relates that a stone was hollowed out by the sobs of the saint who was praying for her father's salvation. The chapelle des Anges [Chapel of the Angels] was built on a projecting rock on the site of a Roman watchtower. A

17th Century sundial bears a Latin inscription: You see how the receding shadow marks the hours; a shadow rules over the shade, we are merely dust and shadow". Inside the convent, you shouldn't forget to stop and admire the stele dating from 1170, which is displayed in the cloister and depicts Saint Odilia receiving the Hohenbourg foundation charter from her father, the Saint's 8th Century tomb, but also those of Etichon and his wife. Also take a look at the chapel where Odilia is buried and its 18th Century paintings, which relate the vicissitudes of the Saint's life

according to the legend. Note also the marquetry Via Dolorosa inside the church, created by Charles Spindler, a famous cabinetmaker artist, in 1934.

Among the numerous walks that one can take from the convent, the most interesting are the following. La source de Sainte Odile [Saint Odilia's Spring]: you can reach this in 20 minutes thanks to the Vosges Club signposts.

It takes little more than 30 minutes to reach the remains of the Niedermunster Monastery. Here you can see the remains of another foundation of Saint Odilia, which included a hospice. The only visible remains are part of the church St Nikolaus of this other foundation which was destined to help the sick and the destitute.

Le mur Païen [Pagan Wall]: It requires several hours to take a tour of this and it is advisable to take a Vosges Club map to ensure that you don't miss anything of this exciting journey across the forest. The best preserved parts are close to the Hagelschloss [Hail Castle] and are 2 to 3 metres high and 1.70 metres thick.

Throughout almost the whole year, the country inn belonging to the Bishopric of Strasbourg welcomes tourists and pilgrims whom it offers board and lodging. The most popular time of the year for visitors is 13 December, Saint Odilia's saint's day.

Heart of the pilgrimage: the sarcophagus containing the embalmed body of the Saint.

23 Champ du Feu

At a height of 1099m, Champ du Feu is a large deforested plateau which was formerly used for stock breeding. From the belvedere tower built by the Vosges Club, there is an all-round view of the Vosges, of the Donon and of the Grand Ballon, as well as of the Alsace plain and the Black Forest. A highly rated cross-country ski resort.

Unspoilt nature: Le Welschbruch.

Pleasures of Winter sports in Strasbourg's nearest resort.

24 Le Struthof Concentration Camp

The only concentration camp to be built on the left bank of the Rhine by the Nazis during the last war, le Struthof has preserved its original structure with its large entrance door, its watchtowers and its double row of barbed wire. Two buildings have been preserved, one of which has been transformed into the Musée de l'Histoire et de la Déportation . Other witnesses of this horror include the cremator building, the prison and the ash pit. Before arriving at the camp, a road leads to a building which was occasionally used as a gas chamber during the Summer of 1943. A large martyr memorial indicates this place from the road which was trodden by more than 8,000 prisoners before the camp evacuation to Dachau in September 1944. The camp itself is overlooked by the national cemetery and by the European Centre of the deported resistant.

So that it is never forgotten …

Le Struthof Concentration Camp and Museum,
F-67130 Natzwiller, Tel: 33(0)3 88 47 44 57, resa.groupes@struthof.fr;
www.struthof.fr, Closed from Christmas to end of February.

Information

25 Barr/Andlau

On the main square, old houses, a fountain and a Renaissance town hall (1610) with voluted gables and a carved balcony provide a typical setting of traditional Alsace, whilst at the back of the square you can make out the outline of the steeple of l'église St Martin. On leaving the square and heading in the direction of the church, a wine path crosses three metres of the vineyard, namely that of Kirschberg, which produces vintage wines. The musée de la Folie Marco constitutes one of Barr's attractions. A poetic 18th Century residence exhibits furniture and earthenware crocker that its owner bequeathed to the

Barr's main square in all its splendour.

Information

Barr Bernstein Inter-communal Tourist Office
*Place de l'Hôtel-de-Ville, F-67140 Barr. Tel: 33(0)3 88 08 66 65
info.tourisme@barr.fr; www.pays-de-barr.com*
Musée de la Folie Marco, *30, rue Stulzer, F-67140 Barr
Tel-Fax: 33(0)3 88 08 94 72*
Andlau Valley Tourist Office, *5, rue du Général de Gaulle,
F-67140 Barr, Tel: 33(0)3 88 08 22 57, www.pays-de-barr.com*

town, together with a vineyard, the wines of which can be tasted in the museum cellar. The nearby Gaensebroenel fountain (geese fountain) has also given its name to one of the region's best wines.

S'Barrestubel, Place de l'Hôtel-de-Ville,
Barr. Tel: 33(0)3 88 08 57 44

Andlau

This wine-growing town owes its rise to the abbey founded by Saint Richardis, wife of Emperor Charles le Gros, around the year 880. Legend has it that a she bear scratching the soil indicated the site of the abbey to Richardis. The convent buildings were destroyed during the Revolution, but l'église Saint Pierre et Saint Paul remains a jewel of primitive Romanesque art. 12th Century remains include the crypt, the portal and a thirty-metre frieze relating typical scenes from daily life and combats. Inside the Church stands the shrine of Saint Richardis and in the crypt a stone she bear, commemorating the sanctuary's origins. Place de l'église is surrounded by beautiful 17th and 18th Century canonical houses. The Renaissance fountain, close to the town hall, is decorated with a statue of Saint Richardis. Two châteaux overlook the town: le Spesbourg and le Haut Andlau. The latter is easily identified by its two powerful cylindrical keeps. It can be reached via the Kastelberg footpath, Kastelberg being the name of both a locality and a Riesling vintage wine.

The shrine of St Richardis.

Au Bœuf Rouge,
6, rue du Dr. Stoltz, Andlau.
Tel: 33(0)3 88 08 96 26

Standing proud, the château overlooks Andlau.

26 Dambach-la-Ville

This is one of the most flowery small towns in Alsace. It is also one of the most important wine-growing communes with its 400 hectares of surrounding land. It has preserved its 14th Century wall, punctuated by three tower gates and a beautiful town hall with cone gables and a fountain, both from the middle of the 16th Century. Whilst taking a stroll, you will see numerous half-timbered or gabled houses decorated with bay windows and signs. The climb to the chapelle Saint

Aerial view of Dambach-la-ville and its marvellous vineyard.

Tourist Office
Townhall, Place du Marché. Tel: 33(0)3 88 92 61 00
otdambach-la-ville@tourisme-alsace.info; www.pays-de-barr.com

A walk not to be missed: the climb to the little Chapel of St. Sebastien.

Sébastien constitutes a delightful walk. The beautiful Baroque altar, situated inside the building, should not be missed. Outside the building is a 16th Century charnel house, undoubtedly from the Peasant War, with the inscription: "Ce que tu es, nous l'avons été" ["We were once what you are now"]. One can return to the ruins of the Bernstein château, the property of the Bishop of Strasbourg, via a signposted footpath. Despite being abandoned subsequent to the Thirty Years' War, and destroyed in 1789, this château has retained its keep and the main part of the building, with its Romanesque windows.

Domaine Ruhlmann, *34, rue du Maréchal Foch · Tel: 33(0)3 88924186 Guided tours of Dambach-la-Ville and its vineyard with le vigneron [wine grower], a little tourist train* **Caveau Nartz** · *12, place du Marché Tel: 33(0)3 88 92 41 11*

These days a rare sight: grape harvesting in the traditional manner.

27 Scherwiller

A small market town with the ruins of the Ortenbourg and Ramstein châteaux as its dominant feature. It is this town that witnessed the end of the Peasant War on 20th May 1529, with the victory of Duke Antoine de Lorraine against 26,000 rebellious Alsatian peasants of whom half were slaughtered. Ravaged by the Swedish in 1634, Scherwiller has nevertheless preserved several old houses, in particular the old 17th Century guardroom with its bay window and carved balcony and the hôtellerie de la Couronne with its courtyard with wooden galleries. The brook which runs through the commune is bordered by picturesque houses, washhouses and lime trees. A quaint custom lives on in this village: houses of a young bride to be are adorned with a heart-shaped roof tile!

L'Ortenbourg shrouded in its autumnal finery.

Scherwiller – Châtenois Tourist Office
2, rue Clémenceau, F-67730
Tel: 33(0)3 88 82 75 00; info@chatenois-scherwiller.net
Visits to Ortenbourg Château the whole year round.

In the flat country of Alsatian Ried, which is frequently flooded by the swellings of the Ill, the three onion dome steeples of Ebersmunster Abbey Church are visible from a long way off. This is the only destroyed during the Thirty Years' War. The original monastery was probably founded in the 7th Century by the father of Saint Odilia, Duke Etichon. The following century it adopted the rule of St Benedict and

Deliciously Baroque: the onion dome steeples of the Abbey as seen from the air.

Baroque church on the left bank of the Rhine. It was built in the 18th Century by Peter Thumb, an architect from Vorarlberg, on the remains of a much older monastery, which was was taken over by the Bishop of Strasbourg. Its earnings rapidly made it into one of Alsace's most important monasteries. The present-day église Saint Maurice [Church of Saint

Abbey church:
www.alsace-visite-guidee.info
Townhall: Tel: 33(0)3 88 85 71 66; www.ebermunster.mairie.com

83

Trompe l'oeil paintings and stuccos: the jubilant atmosphere of the only church of its kind in Alsace.

Maurice] attracts visitors' attention due to its radiance, its trompe l'oeil paintings, its stuccos and its sculptures. Everything focuses on the copiously gilded high altar with its overhanging crown. The cupola of the crossing is covered with paintings by the Tyrolian artist, Joseph Mages, illustrating the life of the Virgin. The organs of André Silbermann, among the best preserved in Alsace, are topped with a fresco representing Saint Cecilia and the musicians. The pulpit is held up by an impressive Samson, created by Clémens Winterhalder. The only remainder of the former monastery is a door surmounted by a painting representing Dagobert, Saint Arbogast and the wild boar. This in fact refers to the tradition of "Ebermunster", which means "monastery of the wild boar", reminiscent of the injury inflicted by a wild boar on one of Dagobert's sons and miraculously healed by Saint Arbogast.

Organs by André Silbermann which form the highly esteemed attraction of the "Musical Hours of Ebersmunster"

29 Sélestat

Its name originates from "scladi-stat", which means "swamp town" and is reminiscent of the fact that Sélestat is situated right in the centre of Ried, this region that is frequently flooded by the waters of the l'Ill.

Residence of the Frankish kings - Charlemagne celebrated Christmas here in 775 - Sélestat became a fief of the Hohenstaufen dynasty at the end of the 11th Century. In the 13th Century, Friedrich II encircled it with high walls, which were destroyed in 1673 by order of Louis XIV, who was anxious to break down the resistance of this important Decapole town. However, in the second half of the 15th Century and the beginning of the 16th Century, Sélestat was witness to particularly brilliant intellectual activity. Its Latin school became the centre of Alsatian humanism, something that is illustrated by the figures of historian, Béatus Rhénanus and reformer, Martin Bucer.

Place du Marché-aux-choux [Cabbage Market Square], rue des Chevaliers [Knights' Street], rue du Babil [Babbling Street], place du Vieux Port [Old Port Square]... just

reading the street names inspires dreams in this very active town – its Tuesday market is very popular and less invaded by tourism than other Alsatian towns and villages. Sélestat has preserved an old and interesting town, with an abundance of picturesque houses overhanging the Tour des Sorcières [Witches' Tower] (1216) and the Tour de l'Horloge [Clock Tower] (1280), the remains of a double belt of fortifications. In spite of the restorations in 1889, l'église Sainte-Foy [the Church of Saint Foy] is one of Alsace's most beautiful Romanesque buildings. The old Holy Sepulchre Chapel which preceded the current church was given to the Conques Abbey, another major stage on the route of this pilgrimage by Hildegarde, widow of Friedrich von Büren. Thus, monks of French culture came from Rouerge to move to Alsace in 1094. In the second half of the 12th Century, they had a new sanctuary built from pink sandstone and grey granite, dedicated to Saint Foy, patron saint of Conques. The apse and the octagonal crossing tower

---

Sélestat Tourist Office
Boulevard du Général Leclerc, BP 90184, F-67604 Sélestat Cedex
Tel: 33(0)3 88 58 87 20/26 – Fax: 33(0)3 88 92 88 63
accueil@selestat-tourisme.com; www.selestat-tourisme.com
Humanist Library *1, rue de la Bibliothèque*
Tel: 33(0)3 88 58 07 20
bibliotheque.humaniste@ville-selestat.fr; www.bibliotheque-humaniste.eu

An impressive concentration of old houses at the foot of the churches of St Foy and St George, next to the Humanist Library.

constitute the oldest parts of the building. The Romanesque façade, which has been much remodelled, is surrounded by two towers, the spires of which date from the 19th Century. Inside, the crypt inspired by that of the Holy Sepulchre in Jerusalem undoubtedly dates back to the original church. Here, you can find a cast of l'Inconnue de Sainte Foy [the Unknown of Saint

Foy], found during excavations, which might represent Hildegarde de Büren.

A few metres from Saint Foy, stands l'église Saint Georges [Church of Saint George], built between the 13th and 15th Century and thus illustrating all developments in Gothic style. On entering, one is struck by the radiance of the stained-glass windows of the choir, which, dating from the 15th Century, represent, like the illuminations, the lives of several saints. The Renaissance pulpit, which is held up by a statue of Samson, is remarkable.

Not far from here stands the Halle aux Blés [Wheat Hall], the first floor of which houses Sélestat's the town of Sélestat dating from the 16th Century, display cabinets of which the garnet-red velvet drapes have to be raised before you can see the precious volumes they hold, straight away lend this large room a special atmosphere. Along the five cabinets, you will discover a 7th Century Merovingian lectionary,

The procession of floral floats in August with its thousands of dahlias: a festival not to be missed.

famous humanist library, which, together with Strasbourg Cathedral and the Issenheim altarpiece, ranks among Alsace's greatest cultural treasures. In fact, its collection comprises two libraries: both the bibliothèque paroissiale [parish library] or bibliothèque de l'école latine de Sélestat [library of Sélestat's Latin School], built up from 1452, and the personal library of the humanist, Béatus Rhénanus, born 1485 in this town. Beautiful mediaeval statues, a relief map of the study books of Béatus Rhénanus, the works of Erasmus of Rotterdam, numerous works printed in Basel and Strasbourg, and not forgetting this curio: the 1507 cosmography of Saint Dié", where the word "America" appears for the first time ever.

Residences likely to attract attention include number 8, rue Bornert, the house where Béatus Rhénanus spent his childhood and the late Renaissance style maison Billex, a place of historic interest: it is in this house that Louis XIV spent the night of 14 October 1681, whilst waiting to receive the surrender of envoys from the town of Strasbourg.

On the road leading to the centre: a water tower characteristic of the period around 1900, reminiscent of art nouveau, remains one of the town's characteristic emblems.

 Au Bon Pichet (Wine Tavern),
10, Place du Marché-aux-Choux.
Tel: 33(0)3 88 82 96 65
Auberge de la Paix,
44, rue Prés Raymond Poincaré.
Tel: 33(0)3 88 92 14 50
La Maison du Pain,
8, rue du Sel. Tel: 33(0)3 88 58 45 90;
www.maisondupain.org
L'Auberge de l'Ill (gastronomic),
2, rue Collonges au Mont d'or,
68970 Illhaeusern.
Tel: 33(0)3 89 71 89 00

A surprise on every corner, just like this little halberdier.

Inside the Humanist Library with the bust of Mentelin.

30 Kintzheim

At the entrance to the village you will see the Willemin Château, which dates back to the end of the 18th Century. Close to the Church and the 15th Century chapelle Saint Jacques [Saint James Chapel], the walls of which are adorned with frescoes. However, the main attraction

A moment of pure happiness.

are a fountain and a pretty wooden house, which was built in 1509. Near to the Haut-Koenigsbourg route, you should make a stop to visit the Kintzheim Château, an impressive 13th and 15th Century construction. The cylindrical keep with its bartizans overhangs the ruins of the home which is perforated with a large number of windows is really the show entitled Volerie des Aigles [Eagles in Flight], which takes place in the courtyard and involves demonstrations of wild birds of prey. Further on and to the right, a road suitable for motor vehicles leads to the old maison forestière de la Wick [de la Wick forest house] and to the Montagne des Singes [Monkey Mount], a 20-hec-

Haut-Koenigsbourg, Kintzheim, Orschwiller Tourist Office
Route de Sélestat. Tel: 33(0)3 88 82 09 90 and 33(0)3 88 82 11 62
ot.kintzheim-orschwiller@evc.net, **Volerie des Aigles.** Tel: 33(0)3 88 92 84 33
www.infoparks.com; promp@voleriedesaigles.com, **Montagne des Singes.**
Tel: 33(0)3 88 92 11 09, www.montagnedessinges.com; info@montagnedessinges.com
Cigoland, amusement park. Tel: 33(0)3 88 92 05 94, www.cigoland.fr; contact@cigoland.fr

All wings spread; the powerful flight of the birds of prey impresses the crowd of spectators.

Macaques have a weakness for popcorn!

tare enclosure which is inhabited by 200 macaques from the Atlas Mountains of Morocco. Perfectly adapted to the harsh Alsatian climate, these very friendly monkeys come to eat popcorn out of visitors' hands, which is sold together with the entrance ticket. Subsequently, return to Kintzheim to walk along the Sélestat route. Another attraction is offered here: le parc des cigognes et des loisirs, which includes llamas, fallow deer and wallabies, as well as a little train, old cars and a mini-golf course, etc. There is something for everyone.

Auberge Saint Martin
80, rue de la Liberté
Tel: 33(0)3 88 82 04 78

31 Haut-Koenigsbourg

Haut-Koenigsbourg Château, *F-67600 Orschwiller - Information (Monday through Friday): Tel: 33(0)3 88 82 50 60, Fax: 33(0)3 88 82 50 61 haut-koenigsbourg@cg67.fr; www.haut-koenigsbourg.fr*
The Château is open every day, except on 1st January, 1st May, 25th December. January, February, November and December: 9:30 am to 12:00 pm and 1:00 pm to 4:30 pm, March and October 9:30 am to 5:00 pm, April, May and September 9:15 am to 5:15 pm, June, July and August 9:15 am to 6:00 pm, Every evening, the Chateau closes 45 minutes after ticketing. - Country Inn, bookstore and souvenir shop: 33(0)3 88 82 37 80, Classed as historic monument in 1993, the administration of the Haut-Koenigsbourg Château was transferred to the Bas-Rhin General Council in 2007.

At a height of over 750 metres, Haut-Koenigsbourg Château overlooks the Rhine plain. The property of Emperor Friedrich 1st of Hohenstaufen and his brother, Konrad, who each shared a tower in the 12th Century, the château was passed down to the Dukes of Lorraine in the middle of the 13th Century, then to the Bishops of Strasbourg a century later. Largely rebuilt at the end of the 15th Century by Oswald and Wilhelm von Thierstein, a Swiss family of counts who can trace their roots back to the Hapsburg dynasty, the château was destroyed by the Swedish during the Thirty Years' war.

The Haut-Koenigsbourg Château was in ruins when it was presented by the town of Sélestat to Emperor Wilhelm II in 1889, who took pains to glorify the Hohenzollern dynasty of which he was a member, as well as to inscribe this in the continuation of the Hohenstaufen and Hapsburg dynasties. He entrusted the architect, Bodo Eberhardt, with the château's restoration. This gentleman was to supervise the building work between the years of 1900 and 1908, after having carried out archaeological research on all the fragments of glass, tiles from tiled stoves, etc. found in the ground, as well as a study of all the other châteaux of the period, not forgetting the archive texts. The result: a fortified château that despite failing to completely recreate its 15th Century incarnation (which was used as a reference), constituted the prototype for a mediaeval fortress and a brilliant educational tool. This interesting sight did not

Restored by Wilhelm II, the Haut-Koenigsbourg fortress remains the unrivalled prototype of a mediaeval fortified château, which inspires thousands of visitors.

Romantic engraving of the Hoh-Koenigsbourg Château.

go unnoticed by tourists, as it is classed as France's most highly visited monuments after the Eiffel Tower and Mont Saint Michel. Nevertheless, it has taken as long as 1993 for this restoration to be classed as a historic monument.

The whole of the château is overlooked by the high quadrangular keep – a symbolic figure for the place – featuring a leather roof topped by a large eagle with spread out wings. You have to pass two walls in order to access the steward buildings, such as the country inn, the stables, forge and mill.

After the drawbridge, the porte des Lions or Lions' gate allows you access to the château. A 62-metre deep fortified well is built on the border of the rocky spur on which the stately home stands. On its ground floor are situated the cellar and the kitchens where one of Alsaces's oldest barrels is kept. The upper floors include the knights' apartments, the guest rooms and the chapel. The most impressive rooms are situated on the West side. Notably the community hall, which has been deco-

rated with frescoes by Léo Schnug, representing the siege of the château in 1462.

The next room is the Chambre Lorraine, which was entirely refurnished by the Haut-Koenigsbourg Verein [Haut-Koenigsbourg Club] with the aim of recreating the spirit of the time. The armoury displays impressive armour and

The Hohenzollern coat of arms surmounted by that of Charles V adorns the façade of the South abode.

Salle du Kaiser [Emperor's Room], also known as the salle des Fêtes [Party Room]. On the vault an eagle spreads his wings in the direction of the Hohenzollern Crowning.

The varnished ceramic tiles, recovered in the excavations, were used to make the wonderful ceramic stoves of a Nuremberg company.

Chambre Lorraine was entirely furnished thanks to donations by the Lorraine Society for History and Archaeology.

knives, in particular formidable crossbows. In this room, an earthenware stove, similar to a model kept in Salzburg Castle attracts the visitor's admiration. It is not the only one, as nearly all the rooms were heated using these stoves. The North part of the living quarters features the marshals' apartments on the first floor and on the second floor the Empress' Suite, built for the wife of Wilhelm II. The Southern part of the living quarters was reserved for the Counts of Thierstein. The chapel is situated next to the bedchamber. This was heated by a chimney and features a real exception for this abode, namely latrines. The next room is a living room with a bay window to let in light and from which there is a magnificent view. After visiting the home, return to the fresh air in the Haut-jardin before climbing to the top of the Great Bastion and its two solid corner towers. From here, where impressive artillery cannons are displayed, there is a striking view of le Grand Ballon, le Hohneck and the neighbouring châteaux of Frankenbourg, Ramstein and Ortenbourg. It is here where the château stands that a famous scene from the 1937 Jean Renoir film "La Grande Illusion", with the actors Pierre Fresnay, Erich von Stroheim and Jean Gabin, was filmed.

Round or square? The question was asked for a long time during the restoration. Finally, the answer: quadrangular, a shape which has been retained and thus the keep stands from the East with the Southern tower of the small bastion.

From far off, Haut-Koenigsbourg watches over the plain which is always invaded by visitors. Both day and night in Summer when mediaeval evenings are organised, which breath life into the old fortress.

32 Ribeauvillé

This town is not only France's smallest subprefecture, but was also the seat of the Ribeaupierre seigneury in the Middle Ages, one of the most powerful families in Alsace. Enclosed by walls at the end of the 13th Century, of its ramparts Riebeauvillé has preser-

A subprefecture at the foot of the three châteaux bordered by the vineyard.

Ribeauvillé and Riquewihr Region Tourist Office, *Ribeauvillé Tourist Reception Office, 1, Grand'Rue, BP 90067, F-58153 Ribeauvillé Cedex, Tel.: 33(0)3 89 73 23 23; Fax: 33(0)3 89 73 23 29*
info@ribeauville-riquewihr.com; www.ribeauville-riquewihr.com
Guided tours of Ribeauvillé in small tourist train, *Tel.: 33(0)3 89 73 24 24 or 73 77 60,*
Casino: *Tel: 33(0)3 89 73 43 43, casinoribeauville@lucienbarriere.com;*
www.lucienbarriere.com, **Vineyard and Viticulture Museum,** *Cave Vinicole de Ribeauvillé [Ribeauvillé wine cellar] 2, Rte de Colmar. Tel: 33(0)3 89 73 61 80*
Town Museum, *Place de la Mairie. Tel: 33(0)3 89 73 20 00,* **Beauvillé factory shop,**
famous fabric print manufacturer, 19, Rte de Ste-Marie-aux-Mines. Tel: 33(0)3 89 73 74 74

The Butchers' Tower overhanging the main square.

ved the two tours des Cigognes [Stork Towers]. The tour des Bouchers [Butchers' Tower] in the town centre overlooks one of the town's four districts, each of which are surrounded by a special wall. This tower from the end of the 13th Century, heightened in the 16th Century, spans la Grand' Rue. On the square which is dominated by the Butchers' Tower flows a Renaissance fountain, surmounted by a small lion with a shield bearing the town coat of arms. On one side stands the 18th Century town hall, which is renowned for its collection of 15th, 16th and 17th Century silver and silver gilt goblets, as well as the region's speciality, beautiful plates for cloth printing, donated to the town by the Ribeaupierre family. On the other side stands the convent church, an old Augustinian church from 1412 with its Gothic portal surmounted by a small rose window. In the pier there is a beautiful Gothic sandstone virgin dating from the 14th Century.

Beyond the Butchers' Tower, la Grand' Rue leads to the place de la Sinne with its fountain. To the right, a street climbs to the Gothic style parish church, built between 1282 and 1473. By following la Grand' Rue, you will pass in front of the old Du Soleil inn with its turret overlooking a courtyard, before reaching la place de la

République and its beautiful Renaissance fountain.

On leaving the Butchers' tower in the opposite direction, to the right you will see the old hospital chapel, the sole vestige of which is the choir.

A little further to the left stands the halle aux Blés or Wheat Hall with its two passages and Gothic portal. From the same side, the Avé Maria house is noted for its bay window decorated with an annunciation. This house is also known as Pfifferhus, in memory of the brotherhood of the strolling fiddlers of Haute Alsace who met at Ribeauvillé every year on 8 September. A tradition which is maintained and constitutes one of Alsace's most popular festivals.

Goblets are overflowing thanks to the town's three well-known vintage wines -le geiberg produces a refined Riesling, l'osterberg is renowned for its Tokay and Gewurtztraminer. That is unless one prefers Carola mineral water for which the factory at the entrance to the town is reputed.

Above the town stand the ruins of the three châteaux of Saint Ulrich, Girsberg and Ribeaupierre. In town, a fourth château, dating from the 17th Century, today houses a secondary school.

The Saint Ulrich Château, the primary residence of the Ribeaupierre family, is the most impressive. It comprises a square keep and a main part of the building from the beginning of the 12th Century. Expansions began from the 13th Century and the

Le Pfiffer de l'an 1300

The first Sunday in September, Ribeauvillé celebrates the strolling fiddlers during "Pfifferdaj" [Pipers' Day], a tradition which dates back to the Middle Ages. The noblemen of Ribeauvillé were official protectors of flute players, strolling players and acrobats who paid homage to them once a year.

Ribeauvillé vineyards produce wines that can be tasted in cellars and restaurants. The Wine Fair is held on the penultimate weekend in July.

in length and lengthened by a small chapel dedicated to Saint Ulrich. Several minutes' walk away, le Girsberg stands with its powerful 13th Century keep with projecting bosses. The same path leads to Haut-Ribeaupierre, a 13th and 14th Century château, the sole remains of which are the crenellated keep and a part of the wall.

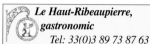

Le Haut-Ribeaupierre,
gastronomic
Tel: 33(0)3 89 73 87 63

Hotel-Restaurant Caveau de l'Ami Fritz
Tel: 33(0)3 89 73 68 11

Hotel-Restaurant Au Valet de Cœur,
gastronomic
40, Rte de Ste-Marie-aux-Mines.
Tel: 33(0)3 89 73 88 78

Legend has it that the Magi stayed in Ribeauvillé, thus giving their name to this 16th Century inn.

château was completed with a further keep, a knights' room 17m

In the foreground, from left to right, the Saint Ulrich Château, which has preserved its square keep and a magnificent knights' room, which faces the Girsberg Château and its pentagonal tower. Haut-Ribeaupierre overhangs them both.

33 Riquewihr

Resting on the hillsides covered with the Schoenenbourg and Sporen vineyards, two 'grand cru' wines, to which it attributes its wealth, Riquewihr is one of the most attractive and highly visited villages in Alsace.

The vineyard hugs the ramparts of the old fortified village.

Ribeauvillé and Riquewihr Region Tourist Office
Riquewihr Tourist Reception Office,
2, rue de la 1ère Armée, BP 90067, F-68153 Ribeauvillé Cedex
Tel.: 33(0)3 89 73 23 23; Fax: 33(0)3 89 73 23 29
info@ribeauville-riquewihr.com; www.ribeauville-riquewihr.com
Musée de la Communication en Alsace [Alsace Communication Museum]
(contains collections from the Diligence [Stagecoach] and Histoire des P.T.T
(P&T History) museums). Tel.: 33(0)3 89 47 93 80; muse@shpta.com;
www.shpta.com, **Hansi Museum,** *16, rue du Général de Gaulle, F-68340*
Tel.: 33(0)3 89 47 97 00, Fax: 33(0)3 89 49 01 20, lemuseehansi@aol.com
Dolder Museum, *rue du Général de Gaulle, F-68340, Tel.: 33(0)3 89 49 08 40,*
Fax: 33(0)3 89 49 08 49, **Musée de la Tour des Voleurs** *[Thieves' Tower] and*
Maison de vigneron (Viticulturist house), rue des Juifs, F-68340,
Tel.: 33(0)3 89 49 08 40, Fax: 33(0)3 89 49 08 49

Riquewihr is best reputed not for the water from its fountain, but for the wines, the vines of which were cultivated on the slopes of Sporen and Schoenenbourg.

← *Porte de Dolder, 25 metres in height, houses the Historical Museum.*

The former property of the princes of Wurtemberg-Montbéliard, this village stretches across the length of the inside of the ramparts and can be visited on foot. To the East, the village can be entered by passing beneath the arch of quite an ordinary 19th Century town hall and one subsequently finds oneself thrusted into a a décor dating from the Middle Ages and the Renaissance.

Riquewihr counts no less than five museums: a record for a small town of 1,200 inhabitants. The first, the Post Museum, is housed in the château of the Wurtemberg–Montbéliards. The Stagecoach Museum itself is situated a little further on, in the former château stables.

Along the whole of the main street is a succession of beautiful dressed stone and half-timbered houses, predominantly dating from the 16th and 17th Century. Beautiful signs brighten up the street, such as those drawn by the famous illustrator, Jean-Jacques Waltz, otherwise known as Hansi (1873-1951), who has a museum dedicated to his works, situated in the beautiful house known as Au Nid de Cigognes [At the Storks' Nest]. You really shouldn't miss the Preiss and Zimmer signs hanging against the sky of Riquewihr, as well as that of Hugel by the

talented painter: one depicts a pot-bellied middle class gentleman, very much in the style of the 1830s, who, in trousers and a large frock coat, invites you to taste Alsatian wine. The other sign represents a family harvesting grapes. Not content with modifying his drawings on paper, Jean-Jacques Waltz was accustomed to making several on-site visits to ensure a perfect balance between his signs and their façades. The visitor cannot fail to admire these little works of art in the open air.

On arriving at the end of the village, you will see the double fortified wall, with a fortified gate from the late 13th Century and the entrance to the Historical Museum (Sound and Light Show in Summer, Fridays at 10.00 p.m.) This is surrounded by a second gate, Obertor or Porte Supérieur [upper gate] which dominates the second 16th Century wall. Close by, the Tour des Voleurs or Thieves' Tower contains a torture chamber which is open to the public.

However, in Riquewihr, you should also take a stroll along the less side streets frequented. With every step you take, you will find yourself faced with a beautiful house, a courtyard, a well, a portal, a fountain or a bay window, all of which are worth a look. Rue des Ecuries [Stables Street] features several 16th Century houses of which one half-timbered house is deemed to be the highest in Alsace. The only vestige in Rue des Trois Eglises [Three Church Street] is the Protestant church, the other sanctuaries of St Erhard and Notre-Dame were transformed into private houses during the Reformation, but have retained traces of their former vocation. At the end of the cour des Juifs [Jewish Courtyard], a former

Don't hesitate to meander down the side streets to discover the treasures they hold in store.

The Stagecoach Museum, situated in the old château stables.

The Musée de l'Histoire des P.T.T. always on the lookout for new exhibitions to surprise its visitors

ghetto, a flight of stairs enables the visitor to climb to the rampart walk and to the Thieves' Tower. Situated in Rue du Cerf [Stag Street], the maison Kiener is decorated with a danse macabre. Opposite is the sign of the former inn, hôtellerie du Cerf – a large life-sized wooden cervid is a mere copy, the original is in the Unterlinden de Colmar Museum.

Finally, you shouldn't depart from Riquewihr without having visited the rue Latérale and the rue de la Première Armée, which are noted for both the former communal baths and the Strasbourg Court-yard.

Riquewihr's reputation for vineyards is well-established: the localities, such as Clos des Sorcières or le Rosenbourg are very popular

A sign drawn by the famous illustrator, Hansi.

Alsatian wines. Vintage season is when it is particularly recommended to visit Riquewihr, which ranks among France's five most visited villages.

Les Caves Hugel et Fils, *3, rue de la 1ère Armée*
Tel: 33(0)3 47 92 15
Au Cep de Vigne, *13, rue du Général de Gaulle, Tel: 33(0)3 47 92 34*
Hotel-Restaurant Le Sarment d'Or, gastronomic
4, rue du Cerf. Tel: 33(0)3 89 86 02 86

Riquewihr, like all other Alsatian villages, like to "dress up" to celebrate Christmas.

Hunawihr

Hunawihr's fortified church is used by two denominations – Catholic and Protestant. It is surrounded by a cemetery, which itself is surrounded by a high wall, reinforced with six semi-circular bastions.

The Church's 15th Century steeple functioned as a keep. Inside, the flamboyant Gothic-style pulpit is an integral part of one of the pillars. To the left of the choir are 15th Century frescoes representing episodes in the life of Saint Nicholas. At the foot of the hill upon which rests the Church, the Huna fountain has a story to tell. One year, when the harvest had been poor,

← Riquewihr: Overlooking the village from on high, the tall 13th Century tower features a belfry, where the old bell still sounds twice a day in honour of the wine shippers.

A village surrounded by vines, overlooked by the steeple keep of its fortified church.

Saint Huna, a relative of Saint Odile, transformed the fountain's water into wine. The whole village rushed up to fill tubs and barrels. Hunawihr also has its own Storks Park, which was set up to promote the reintroduction of waders to Alsace and also has a greenhouse with exotic butterflies.

A settled migrant.

34 Kaysersberg

The Emperor's Mountain owes its name to the fortified château, the round keep of which dominates the town and was raised in the age of the Hohenstaufen dynasty. Two great names are attached to this picturesque town which was one of the ten towns of the Decapole:

The Romanesque portal of the Church of the Holy Cross opens on to a small square decorated with a fountain surmounted by the statue of Emperor Constantine and is well worth a visit.

Information

Kaysersberg Valley, Vineyard and Mountain Tourist Office
39, rue du Général de Gaulle, F-68240 Kaysersberg
Tel: 33(0)3 89 61 30 11; Fax: 33(0)3 89 71 34 11
info@kaysersberg.com; www.kaysersberg.com
Musée d'Histoire locale, *64, rue du Général de Gaulle*
Tel: 33(0)3 89 78 11 11
Albert Schweitzer Museum, *126, rue du Général de Gaulle*
Tel: 33(0)3 89 47 36 55
www.ville-kaysersberg.fr
Its famous Christmas Market

The little oratory stands on the fortified bridge from which one can enjoy a particularly ravishing view of the ruins of the Kaysersberg Château.

Musicologist, writer, doctor, Nobel Peace Prize recipient Albert Schweitzer is the object of a veritable cult in Kaysersberg.

Situated next to his house of birth, a little museum is dedicated to Schweitzer.

Memoirs of Albert Schweitzer

Wooden panel houses with bay windows present a first-class architectural ensemble

Geiler de Kaysersberg, a famous preacher of the Strasbourg Cathedral (1445-1510) and Albert Schweitzer (1875-1965), doctor at Lambaréné in Gabon and winner of the Nobel Peace Prize in 1952.

The view of the château is particularly remarkable from the fortified bridge which stretches across the La Weiss courtyard and comprises a small oratory. The Du Pont inn, a former bathhouse, is situated close by. A little further on, the birth house of Albert Schweitzer is adjacent to a museum that is dedicated to him.

On the place de l'église Saint - Croix [Church of the Holy Cross Square] stands a 15th Century fountain, surmounted with a statue of the Emperor Constantine carrying the cross of Christ. From here, one can enter the church through the main portal which dates from 1230. Its tympanum represents the crowning of the Virgin.

The inside is a veritable museum of mediaeval sculpture. The choir features a shining gilt altarpiece with 14 polychrome reliefs illustrating the life of Christ. This masterpiece of Hans Bongartz de Colmar (1518) is surmounted by statues of Saint Christopher, Saint Helena and Saint Marguerite. The reverse side is adorned with paintings from 1622.

In the North aisle, a Holy Sepulchre from 1514 consists of very moving statues of female saints, a

115

masterpiece of Jacques Wirt. The stomach of Christ is pierced with a gash, destined to receive the wafers during the Holy Week.

Next to the Church, the chapelle St-Michel [Chapel of Saint Michael], a former cemetery chapel, comprises an impressive charnel house with a notable stoup decorated with a death's-head and an inscription declaring "Thus it is good: here the Lord is among peasants". In the small neighbouring cemetery, a plague victims' cross, a lantern of the dead and a bildstoeckel (oratory stele) are worth a look.

The Renaissance town hall (1604) denotes the prosperity of this wine-growing town. The hospital, a former Franciscan monastery, has preserved an flamboyant Gothic cloister. The town museum is situated in a pretty house dating from 1521. Among its curios figure two enormous studded clogs, said to have been worn by a hermit by way of penitence.

Don't leave Kaysersberg without taking a look at the Renaissance well which was built in 1618 and stands in the courtyard of number 54 of Grand' Rue. Here one can read the following inscription: "If you gorge yourself on water at table, this will freeze your stomach; I advise you to drink good, old and fine wine and to leave my water alone". Wise counsel in a town that can pride itself on producing Alsace's first wine to have benefitted from vintage appellation since 1975.

This refers to Schlossberg whose terraced vineyard dominates more than 80 hectares of the town.

Not to be missed during the month of December: the Kaysersberg Christmas market, one of the most authentic in Alsace.

Le Moréote, *12, rue du Général Rieder, F-68240 Kaysersberg Tel: 33(0)3 89 47 39 08*
Hassenforder, *129, rue du Gl de Gaulle. Tel: 33(0)3 89 47 13 54*
Domaine Weinbach, *25, Rte des Vins, Tel: 33(0)3 89 47 13 21; contact@domaineweinbach.com*

The surrounding wall was erected in 1227 by order of Friedrich II.

35 Colmar

A Prefecture of the High Rhine, Colmar, the flowered town, has a total of 68,000 inhabitants.

It was in 823, under Emperor Louis the Pious that the word colombarium appeared for the first time. This was probably a dovecot of the Gallo-Roman town, the modified name of which was subsequently used to describe the whole of Colmar. However, the true rise of Colmar did not really commence until the 13th Century. The first surrounding wall was built in 1220 and some years later, Emperor Friedrich II granted it the

Assembled around the St Martin collegiate church, Vieux Colmar [Old Colmar] and its eternal charm ensure that you don't forget the dynamism of a town famous for its Wine Fair.

Colmar and Region Tourist Office, 4, rue d'Unterlinden F-68000 Colmar, Tel: 33(0)3 89 20 68 92, Fax: 33(0)3 89 41 34 13, info@ot-colmar.fr; www.ot-colmar.fr
Unterlinden Museum, Place d'Unterlinden. Tel: 33(0)3 89 20 16 60, Fax: 33(0)3 89 41 26 22. musees@ville-colmar.com, **Bartholdi Museum**, 30, rue des Marchands, Tel: 33(0)3 89 41 90 60. musees@ville-colmar.com,
Musée animé du Jouet et des petits trains, 40, rue Vauban. Tel: 33(0)3 89 41 93 10, Fax: 33(0)3 89 24 55 26, **Natural History Museum**, 11, rue Turenne. Tel: 33(0)3 89 23 84 15, Fax: 33(0)3 89 41 29 62, shne.colmar@orange.fr; www.museumcolmar.org
Sweet Narcisse, boat sight-seeing rides, 12A, rue de la Herse, Tel: 33(0)3 89 41 01 94, **Regional Tourist Committee, 20A, rue Berthe Molly**, BP 50247, F-58005 Colmar cedex, Tel: 33(0)3 89 24 73 50, Fax: 33(0)3 89 24 73 51, crt@tourisme-alsace.com;
www.tourisme-alsace.com, **Association Départementale du Tourisme du Haut-Rhin** (High Rhine Departmental Tourist Association), Maison du Tourisme Haute-Alsace, F-58006 Colmar-cedex, Tel: 33(0) 89 20 10 68, Fax: 33(0)3 89 23 33 91, adtpromotion@tourisme68.com; www.tourisme68.com

title and privileges of an imperial town.

After Alsace was reattached to France, Colmar became the seat of the Sovereign Council of Alsace, a court of justice which exercised its jurisdiction over the whole of the province. That is why, even today, Strasbourg is still dependent on the Colmar court of appeal. During the Napoleonic era, Colmar distinguished itself by nine generals who were natives of the town. Among them: General Rapp, who gave his name to one of the main squares. Other famous personages include the great painter, Martin Schongauer (1450-1491), August Bartholdi (1834-1904), the sculptor of the Statue of Liberty in New York and the illustrator, Jean-Jacques Waltz, otherwise known as Hansi (1873-1951).

A visit to Colmar begins with the

Unterlinden convent cloister one of France's most popular museums.

Unterlinden Museum, one of France's great museums which is based in the former Dominican

Lively and very commercial, Colmar centre can mostly be visited on foot, which makes a very pretty round walk.

The Issenheim altarpiece, painted by Mathias Grünewald around 1515. Closed it shows a dramatic crucifixion.

convent, founded in the 13th Century. This convent was a religious home of great and mystic fervour in the 14th and 15th Centuries. The entrance to the museum can be found on the place d'Unterlinden. The first thing you will see is the Alsatian early masters, represented by three great artists: Mathias Grünewald, Martin Schongauer and Gaspart Isenmann.

You will linger in front of the altarpiece painted around 1515 by Grünewald for the Issenheim Antonite Monastery. This charitable order tended to the illness of those suffering from St Anthony's Fire. The work includes eleven panels that can be opened differently according to the liturgical calendar. The large central panel realistically represents the death of Christ. Both the brilliance of colours and the facial expressions make this work into an unforgettable representation of the bitterest pain. A glorious and luminous resurrection and the apocalyptic Temptation of Saint Anthony can also be seen. The sculpted wooden altar, which supports the altarpiece, is decorated with three large statues by Nicolas of Haguenau: Saint Anthony, Saint Augustine and Saint Jerome.

The work of Martin Schongauer, filled with tenderness and harmony, forms a striking contrast to that of Grünewald, about thirty years his junior. Having listed these masters of Rhenish painting, one can not fail to admire the framework in which they are exhibited: The Dominican Chapel, built in the mid-13th Century and the cloister from the same period with its 16th Century "wine well". The Museum contains many other treasures, which range from archaeological collections to contemporary painting.

Close by, opposite the theatre, stands the former 14th Century Saint Catherine Convent, transformed in the 18th Century, which has preserved its cloister and part of its old church with its beautiful 18th Century ceiling.

Behind the Convent, you can follow the rue des Boulangers, bordered by old houses, but not without having beforehand taken several steps along the rue des Têtes to see the house of the same name, which is Colmar's most beautiful Renaissance residence, with its 106 grimaces. From rue des Boulangers you will reach rue Berthe Molly, where, next to number 10, an 18th Century house where Voltaire lived, a courtyard opens up, which is bordered by a beautiful 1598 wooden gallery. Retrace your steps. To the right, Rue des Boulangers runs into place des Dominicains [Dominicans Square].

The Dominican Church, from the end of the 13th Century, the choir

The Maison des Têtes [House of Heads] built around 1608 owes its name to the sculpted heads on the two-floor-high bay window which adorns the façade. A sculpture depicting a cooper stands on the top. It was created by Auguste Bartholdi around 1902

of which dates back to the 15th Century, contains splendid 14th and 15th Century stained glass windows and 18th Century stalls. The real attraction is inside, one of Martin Schongauer's works of art, the Virgin and the Rose Bush.

Next door, the library, with one of the richest collections in France, is based in the monastery buildings around a large 15th Century cloister, decorated with murals from the same period.

Via rue des Serruriers, with its beautiful corbelled houses, you can reach the 13th and 14th Century église Saint Martin. Entirely built of yellow sandstone, 73 metres in length, 24 metres wide and 21 metres high, this Church is the largest in the High Rhine department. The portal of the main façade is adorned with a tympanum featuring the Adoration of the Magi, surmounted by a Last Judgement. On the North portal, the tympanum represents an episode in the life of Saint Nicholas, surmounted by a Resurrection of the dead. At the top of the rib of the porch, God sits enthroned, surrounded by fourteen people: musicians, bishop, kings, and angels. To the left, one can make out the signature of "Maitre Humbert", one of the Church's project managers. To the South of St Martin's Church stands a group of beautiful old houses: the former guardroom with its beautiful Renaissance portal and its loggia from the end of the 16th Century, the maison Adolph, the oldest house in Colmar, as well as its ground floor were redone in the 16th Century

On the place de l'Ancienne-Douane [Old Customs Square] stands the fountain created in 1897 by Bartholdi with its bronze sculpture of imperial general, Lazare Schwendi.

Maison Pfister, built 1537, is decorated with medallions and arabesques.

and the third floor was added in the 17th Century. On the corner of rue des Marchands, maison Pfister dates back to 1537. Rue des Marchands [Shopkeepers' Street] is bordered by old houses: number 30, Bartholdi's house of birth, contains a museum dedicated to the sculptor, number 32 maison à la Rose du XVI siècle, number 36, maison de la Viole du XV siècle where Schongauer is reputed to have been born and in rue Schongauer, number 2, maison du Cygne, where he supposedly had his studio. Rue des Marchands ends with a beautiful ensemble of wooden panel houses and leads to l'Ancienne Douane or Koïfhus from 1480, Colmar's economic centre in the 16th Century. Opposite the Koïfhus, on place de l'Ancienne Douane, stands the fountain with the statue created by Bartholdi de Lazare de Schwendi, importer of the Tokay vine to Alsace. One of the façades of the Koïfhus overlooks the place du Marché-aux-Fruits, where you can see the maison Kern from the Renaissance and the old Palais du Conseil Soverain d'Alsace [Court of the Sovereign Council of Alsace], which was built in 1771 and today houses the civil court. Rue des Tanneurs leads to a district of the same name, the restoration of which is most remarka-

ble. Cross the River Lauch and follow the quay, then the rue de la Poissonnerie, bordered by picturesque boatmen's houses. Here is the gateway to the district of Petite Venise with its old houses on the bank of the river. The pont Saint Pierre offers a very beautiful view, illuminated in the evening, of this peaceful part of Colmar. On the corner of the Lauch and of boulevard Saint Pierre are still some remains of the 13th Century ramparts. The rue du Manège runs alongside the Bartholdi Lycée, that is the old Jesuit Monastery, and comes out on the place des Six-Montagnes-Noires. Close by, number 8 of rue des Blés was the hotel du Châpitre de Bâle in the 18th Century. Turn into the Grand'-Rue and admire its 18th Century houses, numbers 74 and 76. Then, turn to the right, where you will find the rue Saint Jean, which you can follow up until the Ancienne Douane by passing in front of the Chevaliers de Saint-Jean Hotel with its two superimposed galleries (1608). Walk back along the Grand'-Rue and past the Ancienne Douane [Former Customs Office]. To the left, on the corner of rue de l'Eglise [Church Street], you will notice a Renaissance house with a bay window decorated with sculptures. On the other side stands the

An incredible concentration of wonderfully preserved half-timbered houses: Colmar is a feast for the photographer's eye!

125

maison des Arcades [House of Archways] – of which there are 10 – with two octagonal towers at its corners (1608). A little further on stands the 14th and 15th [Hunter's Street] leads to place Jeanne d'Arc [Joan of Arc Square], which has preserved several old houses. Nearby, at number 7 of rue Vauban, stands the house of the

In a boat, it's a lot nicer! In July-August, don't hesitate to enjoy one of the organised boat tours on the canals.

Century église des Franciscains [Franciscan Church] with its impressive jube decorated with a wooden crucifix from the beginning of the 16th Century.

Behind the Church, on place du 2 Février [2nd February Square], stands the façade of the former hospital. Rue du Chasseur former Ploughmen's Guild with its sculpted portal from 1626. The rue des Clefs [Street of Keys] passes in front of the town hall, which is housed by the old hotel of the Pairis Abbey from the end of the 18th Century and leads to the Unterlinden Museum, departure point for this route.

De la Vigne à l'Assiette,
  14, Place de l'Ecole
      Tel: 33(0)3 89 23 32 49
La Maison Rouge, *9, rue des Ecoles*
Tel: 33(0)3 89 23 53 22
Aux Amis de la Lauch,
80, Chemin du Lauchwerb
Tel: 33(0)3 89 41 88 32

Aux Trois Poissons, *15, Quai de la*
Poissonnerie
Tel: 33(0)3 89 41 25 21
Le Jardin du Caveau St-Jean,
47, Grand'Rue, Tel: 33(0)3 89 34 09 73
Le Rendez-vous de Chasse, Grand-Hôtel
Bristol, *7, Place de la Gare.*
Tel:; 33(0)3 89 41 10 10

The old market gardeners' quarter which certainly merits its name of Petite Venise.

36 Turckheim

Having belonged to Munster Abbey, Turckheim emancipated itself to become an imperial town in 1312 and some years later a member of the Decapole, a league of ten Alsatian towns. Having passed the main entrance, the Porte de France [Gate of France] surmounted with a stork's nest, one finds oneself on a small square decorated with a fountain topped with an 18th Century Virgin and child. Nearby stands the former 16th Century guardroom. Just as in the Middle Ages, this house remains the starting point for the patrols of the nightwatchman, who, wearing a tricorn and bearing a lantern and a halberd, carries out his patrols during the tourist season every evening at 10.00 p.m. Turckheim has preserved its three mediaeval gates,

Entrance to Turkheim – the 14th Century porte de France [Gate of France] is surmounted by a traditional stork's nest.

 Turckheim and Region Tourist Office
Guardroom. Tel: 33(0)3 89 27 38 44, Fax: 33(0)3 89 80 83 22
www.turckheim-alsace.com

An imposing town hall with its typical Renaissance-style voluted gable.

part of its walls, an imposing town hall from 1595 and a church which has preserved its Romanesque-Gothic steeple, adorned with a gilt cask and a star-shaped weather-cock, symbol of the coopers. Near to the Porte de Munster [Munster Gate], stands a monument in memory of the victory of Toueraient over the imperial army in 1675. As for the Porte de Brand, this bears the name of the vintage wine produced in the vineyard that is a dominant feature of the town. While wandering through the main street and the alleyways of Turck-heim, you will discover many hou-ses with carved beams, in particular the Deux Clefs hotel, an old tavern dating from 1630.

You should also visit Hohlands-bourg château on the route of the five châteaux between Wintzen-heim and Eguisheim. The building of this former fief of Hapsburg commenced in 1279 and the sole remains are curtain walls pierced with arrow slits, which escaped destruction during the Thirty Years' Wars (open everyday from 1 July to mid-September, 10 a.m. to 7 p.m.)

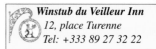

Winstub du Veilleur Inn
12, place Turenne
Tel: +333 89 27 32 22

37 Eguisheim

Village built in concentric circles around what was once the château of the renowned des Eguisheim family, into which Leon IX, pope between 1048 and 1054, was born. Before even entering this village, it is recommended that you take a tour of the ramparts, a splendid walk back in time. On the main square stand the château and the church. The sole remains of the original château are vestiges of the dressed stone wall, the other parts – palace and chapel – were rebuilt in the 19th Century. Dating back to the same era, the rebuilt church has nevertheless preserved a yellow sandstone Romanesque steeple and inside a 13th Century tympanum, representing Christ as King surrounded by St Peter and St Paul and above the retinue wise and insane virgins. As for the rest: Take a stroll in town along the streets bordered with old half-

A village curved around its own château, just like a large cat! A signposted round walk marks out the route of the ramparts.

Eguisheim and Region Tourist Office,
22a, Grand'Rue, F-68420 Eguisheim
Tel: 33(0)3 89 23 40 33, Fax: 33(0)3 89 41 86 20
info@ot-eguisheim.fr; www.ot-eguisheim.fr
Guided tours of Eguisheim in little tourist train.

A native of Eguisheim, Leon IX, history's only Alsatian pope, stands atop the town's main fountain.

131

Attractive signs make the gourmand's mouth water.

timbered houses and beautiful tithe houses, the construction of which stretches between the 16th and the 18th Century. At the street entrances appear beautiful fountains like that of the Virgin (1542) on the small market square. However, it is wine rather than water for which Eguisheim, whose vineyard is one of the largest in Alsace and stretches out across 300 hectares, is renowned.

Three châteaux overhang the town: Weckmund, Wahlenbourg and Dagsbourg, built between the 11th and 13th Century by the Counts of Eguisheim (permanently open to the public, except during bad weather).

Caveau d'Eguisheim Restaurant
3, place du Château St Léon
Tel: +333 89 41 08 89

Three châteaux overhang the little vine town Husseren-les-châteaux:
Weckmund and Walhenbourg enclosed by a commune wall built by the Eguisheim
Counts between the 11th and 13th Century.

38 Munster - Col de la Schlucht

The town owes its name to a Benedictine abbey founded in the 7th Century by the disciples of Saint Gregory the Great. Thus a monastery became a minster. Apart from the market place, there are few vestiges of the past in a town, 85% of which was destroyed during the Second World War. However, la Grande Rue [main street] bordered with shops is still very lively. On the square, the town

At the end of the market place stands the pink sandstone Protestant church, a Neoromanesque-style construction built between 1867 and 1873.

Munster Tourist Office, 1, rue du Couvent, F-68140 Munster
Tel: 33(0)3 89 77 31 80, Fax: 33(0)3 89 77 07 17,
tourisme.munster@wanadoo.fr, **Maison du Parc Naturel Régional des Ballons des Vosges** 1, Cour de l'Abbaye, Tel: 33(0)3 89 77 90 34, Fax: 33(0)3 89 77 90 30, www.parc-ballons-vosges.fr

Information

The countryside of the high mountains, near to "Schiessrothried".

Very welcome stops: the farm inns.

hall from 1550 is decorated with a two-headed eagle, reminding us that Munster formed part of the Decapole and of the Holy Roman German Empire. Another historical reference: the lion fountain dating from 1576, which touches on the right of a population, up to then dominated by the Abbey, to freely practice the Protestant religion. On the edge of the square, the remaining wing of the former abbey palace, which has now become the seat of the Ballons d'Alsace

Regional Nature Park, where you can visit a permanent exhibition. The famous Munster cheese, produced in the valley of the same name, has been known by this name since the 16th Century, although its production dates back to the 9th Century. Nearby on the route des Crêtes is the Col de la Schlucht [Ravine Col], 1,139 metres at its highest point and the highest col of the Vosges. This is a popular centre for Winter sports.

The D417 that crosses the col was built between 1842 and 1869 and was used as drill ground for the troops of Emperor Wilhelm II.

Hotel-Restaurant Verte Vallée,
Parc de la Flecht.
Tel: 33(0)3 89 77 15 15
Aux Abeilles, 26, Rte de Gunsbach.
Tel: 33(0)3 89 77 39 34
Ferme-Auberge de Lameysberg,
F-68380 Breitenbach,
Tel: 33(0)3 89 77 35 30
Ferme-Auberge du Kastelberg, Chemin du
Kastelberg, F-68380 Mittlach
Tel: 33(0)3 89 77 62 25

Alpine skiing, cross-country skiing, snowshoe-walking … all Winter sports can be practiced in the Vosges when snow carpets the ground.

39 Neuf-Brisach

The town of Neuf-Brisach, classed as UNESCO Heritage, was created from 1698, subsequent to the Treaty of Ryswick, which obliged Louis XIV to give up Vieux-Brisach [Old Brisach] (today Breisach am Rhein in Germany) to the Empire. For that reason, the King put Sebastien le Prestre, Lord of Vauban (1633-1707) in charge of building a new fortified town, intended to prevent people crossing the Rhine to this place. Of course, this was given the name of Neuf-Brisach [New Brisach]. It has an octagonal appearance and is surrounded by bastioned ramparts which form the shape of a star.

A walk along the ramparts can be taken from the Belfort Gate (South), where the Vauban Museum is based, to the Colmar Gate (North).

Intercommunical Tourist Office of the Banks of the Rhine
6, Place d'Armes, F-68600 Neuf-Brisach
Tel: 33(0)3 89 72 56 66, Fax: 33(0)3 89 72 91 73
info@tourisme-rhin.com; www.tourisme-rhin.com
Vauban Museum, *7, Place Porte de Belfort.*
Tel: 33(0)3 89 72 93 03 93, info@tourisme-rhin.com; www.tourisme-rhin.com

40 Rouffach

The town developed around Isenbourg Château, one of the residences of the Merovingian kings. The present-day building dates from the 19th Century, but has preserved a very old wine cellar. Housing a façade and its rose window are simply outstanding. One of the two towers has remained uncompleted, whilst the other dates from the 19th Century. Take a tour of the church to see the two doors of the side faç-

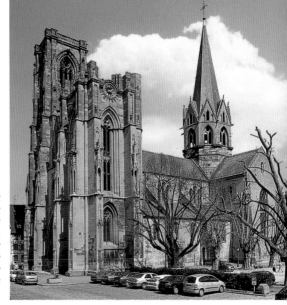

Rouffach's Eglise Notre-Dame de l'Assomption [Our Lady of the Assumption Church] with its unique tower dating back to the 19th Century. The second church was never completed.

gourmet hotel-restaurant, it still overlooks the town from its hill planted with vineyards.

L'église Notre-Dame ranks among Alsace's very beautiful Gothic churches, but has preserved a transept and two Romanesque-style apses from a former building. The ades and the elegance of the Gothic apse which stands in contrast to the silhouette of the Romanesque apsidal chapels. Inside, the nave thrusts up into the light. A 15th Century canopy rises up almost as far as the vault and houses a Virgin from the same period. At the entrance to the

Rouffach Township Tourist Office, *12A, Place de la République, F-68250 Rouffach, Tel: 33(0)3 89 78 53 15, Fax: 33(0)3 89 49 75 30 info@ot-rouffach.com; www.ot-rouffach.com*

choir, two 14th Century staircases mark here and there the location of a missing jube. The stalls date from the 18th Century. You can still see the baptismal fonts from the end of the 15th Century, the tomb of the chevalier au merle was designed by the 14th Century sculptor, Woelflin de Rouffach and to the left of the high altar is a 15th Century canopied tabernacle. The story goes that for a long time in Rouffach the women had been sitting on the right-hand side of the church, which was traditionally reserved for men. This was in memory of an event which had occurred in the Middle Ages. On Easter Sunday of 1106, the assistant provost marshal of the château had a pretty girl kidnapped from Rouffach. The men did not dare react; armed with scythes and pruning knives the women threw themselves into the attack of the château and overpowered the garrison, resulting in the release of the young girl. Another woman of Rouffach is a famous halfwit, better known by the name of Madame Sans-Gêne and the wife of Marshal Lefebvre, who was born at number 1, rue de la Poterne. A monument has been erected in honour of this Napoleonic marshal on the place Clemenceau.

On the other side of place de l'église stands the halle aux Blés from 1569 with its double staircase and stepped gable. Together with the former double-gable town hall this forms a beautiful Renaissance ensemble overlooked by the tour des Sorcières, the remainder of the 14th Century fortifications. This harmonious ensemble makes up one of the most enchanting squares in Alsace.

Rouffach also boasts many 17th Century houses, in particular numbers 11, 17, 23 and 65 of rue du 4eSpahis-Marocains. Why not also take a look at the former 13th Century synagogue, which was remodelled in the 15th Century. The former 15th Century Franciscan convent church with its exterior pulpit houses numerous pieces of armour from the 14th and 18th Centuries.

Since the 19th Century, Rouffach has been home to a school of viticulture which is reputed for its Vorburg vintage wine and its July wine fair.

41 Guebwiller/Murbach

The entrance to this textile town stretches across long terraces of pink sandstone on the slopes of the Lauch Valley and is marked in the East by the impressive and solemn buildings of the region's industry. However, Guebwiller owes its birth and development to Murbach Abbey. Built between 1766 and 1785, l'église Notre-Dame is typi-

St Leger Church is a beautiful example of late Romanesque-style architecture with its Lombard-Rhenish décor.

Guebwiller and Florival Region Tourist Office, *Information Office at Guebwiller, 73, rue de la République, F-68500 Guebwiller. Tel: 33(0)3 89 76 10 63,* **Information Office at Soultz,** *14 Place de la République, F-68360 Soultz, Tel: 33(0)3 89 76 83 60, info@tourisme-guebwiller.fr; www.tourisme-guebwiller.fr*
Florival Museum, *1, rue du 4 Février. Tel: 33(0)3 89 74 22 89 musee-florival-guebwiller@wanadoo.fr,* **Murbach Abbey Church.** *Tel: 33(0)3 89 76 10 63, Check out the www.tourisme-guebwiller.fr website*

An industrial wine-growing town, Guebwiller stretches out lengthways and has a pleasant pedestrian centre.

cal of Alsace's neoclassical buildings. Inside the Church there are remarkable stalls as well as a high altar dedicated to the Assumption of the Blessed Virgin. The tomb of Casimir de Rathsamhausen, prince-bishop of Murbach and founder of the Church, is kept in the crypt. Here and there in the sanctuary are lines of canonical houses which were previously inhabited by the canons of Murbach, who settled in Guebwiller from the 18th Century. A change of décor: the former Dominican Church is Gothic. It has preserved its jube as well as beautiful frescoes. The whole building has become a Musical Training Centre which is open to the public. L'église Saint-Léger [Saint Leger Church] represents a return to Romanesque style, as its portal is a model of this genre. Inside, one can still see the rope and wooden ladders that the Armagnacs used in an attempt to capture the town in 1445. The attacks were fought off thanks to the vigilance and cunning of Brigitte Schick, who lit a straw fire at the place where the town was besieged, leading the enemy to believe in a large-scale counterattack. Like numerous other Alsatian towns, the town hall is a veritable jewel with its 1514 bay window.

Whilst taking a stroll, you will also discover some beautiful mediaeval and Renaissance houses (rue de la République, rue des Blés, etc…) Murbach's abbey church remains one of the most beautiful Romanesque monuments in Alsace, despite the fact the sole remains are the choir and the transept surmounted with two towers. The visitor will admire both the harmony of the forms and the skilful gradation of this building's pink and white sandstone roofing. Note the numerous animal themes developed in the façade, such as the hares that are being bludgeoned by a hunter, whilst two other hares are placing a rope around the neck of another hunter whose hands are tied behind his back.

Murbach: Alsace's oldest Benedictine abbey continues to stand out in the surrounding greenery

The town of Thann developed at the end of the 13th Century at the entrance to the Thur Valley. At this time, the counts of Ferrette, lords in this region, had the Engelbourg Château built, which relics of Saint Theobald. The abundance of pilgrims led to the construction of a collegiate church (1320-1516). Built in pink Soultz sandstone and yellow Rouffach sandstone, this ranks

Thann, the Gothic Church and the Witches' Tower.

was demolished by Louvois in 1673. The sole remains are a circular keep which slopes sideways, thus earning it the nickname of d'oeil de sorcière or Witch's Eye. Situated on a major route linking the North to Italy and the Rhine region to Flanders, Thann became a bastion of pilgrimage around the among the most beautiful Gothic churches of the Rhine valley. A saying states that "Strasbourg steeple is the highest, that of Freiburg im Brisgau the widest and that of Thann the most beautiful". Its portal includes 150 lively scenes of more than 500 characters. Inside, a chapel displays a

Thann Region Tourist Office, *7, rue de la 1ère Armée, F-68800 Thann. Tel: 33(0)3 89 37 96 20, Fax: 33(0)3 89 37 04 58 contact@ot-thann.fr; www.ot-thann.fr*

Information

The large portal of the Collegiate Church of St Theobald displays marvellous sculpted stones.

picturesque Virgin of the Wine Growers. On leaving the collegiate church by the Northern portal, you will notice a beautiful Gothic fountain dedicated to St Theobald, whose legend is re-enacted every year on 30 June, during the great festival of the Cremation of the Three Fir Trees.

The exit to the Tour des Sorcières is the start of the Alsace Wine Route. Thann is where the Rangen vintage wine is produced, on this volcanic rock ground.

143

43 Le Grand Ballon

Le Grand Ballon can be reached on foot (100m from the car park). From the highest summit of the Vosges (1,424m), you will discover an amazing panorama which extends right to the Alps on a clear day. A panoramic table enables you to identify the summits which stretch out of sight. Walking routes (three quarters of an hour) or hikes (three to four hours) are offered around the summit. The descent towards Amic Col, named for a captain who was killed there during the Great War, plunges towards the Thur Valley and the Rossberg. The route overhangs the Vieil-Armand or Hartmannswillerkopf battlefield, which is classed as a historic monument. At the Silberloch Col, a monument commemorates the terrible sacrifice that this geographical spot was forced to make, during the battles of the armies between 1914 and 1918. This war cost a great many human lives, to be precise a total of 30,000 men.

From the Grand Ballon: the highest summit of the Vosges, the view extends right to the Black Forest and the Alps. The Ballon's name originates from the celu of the Celtic god Bel.

44 Le Ballon d'Alsace

Situated at an altitude of 1,247 metres, Ballon d'Alsace has developed into a major tourist location, in Winter as in Summer, where people partake in Nordic skiing, walks with snowshoes, paragliding and hang-gliding. For extends right to the Alps on a clear day. There are two symbolic monuments in memory of the two wars. A statue of Joan of Arc was erected in 1909, when Alsace and Lorraine were reconnected to Germany. A monument of the

At an altitude of 1276m, the Virgin watches over the countryside from the summit of the Petit Ballon. In the background: the Alps.

walkers, it offers an easy excursion to the summit where a statue of the Virgin was erected in 1860. This overlooks the departments of High Rhine, the Bellfort area, Haute Saône and the Vosges, thus offering a panorama which bomb disposal experts in memory of those who lost their lives while removing landmines in the aftermath of the last war. Today classed as a major national attraction, Ballon d'Alsace is under natural protection.

The romantic Vosges

Mulhouse is the second largest city in Alsace and has a total of 120,000 inhabitants.

In German Mühle means mill. Mulhouse owes its name to a mill surrounded by houses, owned by the Strasbourg Abbey of Saint-Etienne, on the banks of the Ill. Imperial town and member of the Decapole, then free town, Mulhouse concluded an alliance with its Swiss neighbours in 1515 and

On place de la Réunion, the Rhenish Renaissance-style town hall is an eyecatcher due to its painted trompe l'œil façade.

Mulhouse Region Tourist Office and Convention Centre, *Avenue Foch, F-68100 Mulhouse, Tel: 33(0)3 89 35 48 48 6 Fax/ 33(0)3 89 45 66 16 info@tourisme-mulhouse.com; www.tourisme-mulhouse.com* **Automobile Town, National Museum – Schlumpf Collection,** *192, Av. de Colmar, F-68100 Mulhouse, Tel: 33(0)3 89 33 23 23, Fax: 33(0)3 89 32 08 09, www.collection-schlumpf.com,* **Train Town, French Railway Museum,** *2, rue Alfred de Glehn, F-68200 Mulhouse. Tel: 33(0)3 89 42 83 33. www.citedutrain.com* **Cloth Printing Museum,** *14, rue Jean-Jacques Henner, F-68100 Mulhouse. Tel: 33(0)3 89 46 83 00, Fax: 33(0)3 89 46 83 10, accueil@musee-impression.com; www.musee-impression.com,* **EDF Electropolis Museum – The Electricity Adventure** *55, rue du Pâturage, F-68200 Mulhouse, Tel: 33(0)3 89 32 48 50, Fax: 33(0)3 89 32 82 47, electropolis@electropolis.tm.fr; www.electropolis.tm.fr,* **Museum of Fine Arts,** *4, Place Guillaume Tell, F-68100 Mulhouse, Tel: 33(0)3 89 33 78 11, Fax: 33(0)3 89 33 78 08, joel.delaine@ville-mulhouse.com; www.mulhouse.fr* **Printed Wallpaper Museum,** *28, rue Zuber, F-68170 Rixheim, Tel: 33(0)3 89 64 24 56, Fax: 33(0)3 89 54 33 06, musee.papier.peint@wanadoo.fr; www.museepapierpeint.org* **Zoological and Botanical Park,** *51, rue du Jardin Zoologique, F-68100 Mulhouse Tel: 33(0)3 89 31 85 10, Fax: 33(0)3 89 31 85 26, zoomulhouse@agglo-mulhouse.fr; www.zoo-mulhouse.com*

A town which has succeeded in combining a rich historic centre with an industrial heritage, which has been converted into prestigious museums..

became French in 1798, only subsequent to a deliberated choice of its bourgeoisie. In the mid-18th Century three citizens of Mulhouse, Dolfus, Koechlin and Schmaltzer begain making painted cloth, otherwise known as printed calico, which had up until then been imported from Switzerland. This was the start of the Alsatian textiles industry. In 1904, the discovery of an important potash deposit near Cernay promoted the development of the chemical industry.

Mulhouse is today a large industrial town, of which the place de l'Europe has become the centre. The view from the top of the tower, extends across the city and its surroundings. The heart of old Mulhouse unfurls around the place de la Réunion, with its town hall. On one of the façades hangs a copy of the famous "Klapperstei" gossips' stone, which was hung around the neck of slanderers before making them cross the city on market day. The original stone, which was used until 1781, is in the historical museum in town hall.

On the square, the 19th Century Protestant Church of Saint-Etienne contains very beautiful 14th Century stained-glass windows and 17th Century stalls.

Opposite the Church, the maison Mieg with its Renaissance turret dates from the 15th Century. The house standing on the corner of rue des Boulangers dates from the mid-17th Century. On the place Lambert, in the direct vicinity, remain two old houses – number 1 and number 5.

In the Grand'Rue, you should take a look at the 14th and 15th Century Saint-Jean chapel, formerly a chapel of the Knights of Malta. It is only open for concerts. Nearby stand the Tour du Diable and the Tour Nessel, remains of the former chateau of the bishops of Strasbourg. Of its fortified surrounding wall, Mulhouse has only preserved its 14th Century Tour du Bollwerk, which is not far from the place de l'Europe.

Mulhouse is the European Capital of Technical Museums. The most important include: the musée de l'impression sur étoffes [Cloth-prin-

Standing firm on the fountain, a stone halberdier remains impassive in the midst of the town's hustle and bustle.

Entirely reconstructed in the 19th Century on the site of a church of the same name, the Church of St Etienne has managed to preserve its stained glass windows from the first church, which are among the most beautiful in Alsace.

ting Museum], which is close to the station; the foremost textile collection in the world, more than 6 million motifs, "indian" cloths of the 18th and 19th centuries, toiles de Jouy, painted fabrics from the whole world, printing machines that can be seen under operation. Almost 50,000 textile documents are displayed during temporary exhibitions. Situated in a beautiful residence (the Villa Steinbach) from the end of the 18th century, the Musée des Beaux Arts [Museum of Fine Arts] presents collections from different schools and eras, works by Pieter Bruegel le Jeune, Teniers, Ruysdael, Boucher, Courbet, Jean-Jacques Henner, an alsatian painter, along with a rich collection from the 19th Century, contemporary art as well as the Artothèque (Art Library) from which art books can be borrowed. The Train Town, having the most beautiful collection of the trains of Europe, will enthusiast all those

Collected by the Schlumpf brothers, the world's largest collection of cars, in a setting that enhances their prestige: interactive audio-guided tour.
Revive the emotions of passengers in the Roaring Twenties, in the largest European railway museum.

Dedicated to the electric fairy, the Electropolis Museum is a hair-raising experience!

Dream of travelling at the Railway Museum which sums up one hundred and fifty years in the history of rail travel.

that dream of trains. In an immense animated space area, it relates more than a century and a half of railway history in France. You can see the car in which Général de Gaulle travelled, the Orient-Express, the Train Bleu that inspired Agatha Christie, decorated with Lalique glass panels, etc., as well as a collection of steam engines.

The Automobile Town extends over 25,000 m² with more than 600 cars,

A bucolic view of the city, with the Tower of Europe in the background, topped with its dome which houses a revolving restaurant.

of which almost 400 historic models are permanently presented: Bugatti, Maserati, Ferrari, Rolls-Royce, Hispano-Suiza, Mercedes, Panhard, Peugeot, Renault, Citroen show the adventure of cars. Here are specially the Bugatti «Royale Type 41» and the Rolls-Royce «Silver Ghost». No doupt the most spectacular car of the year 1921, and also one of the oldest models, the «Type A 1» of Panhard & Levassor out of the year 1898.

If, after having visited all these museums, the visitor wishes to take a walk in the fresh air, he should make his way to the Zoological Park, which has been set up at Rebberg on the site of an old vineyard to the South of the town.

La Table de la Fonderie,
21, rue du Manège.
Tel: 33(0)3 89 46 22 74
L'Essentiel, *5, rue Bonbonnière.*
Tel: 33(0)3 89 66 36 98
Acropolis, *49, rue d'Illzach.*
Tel: 33(0)3 89 42 09 26
La Tour d'Europe, *3, Bd de l'Europe.*
Tel: 33(0)3 89 45 12 14
Auberge alsacienne du Parc zoologique, *31, Av. de la 9e DIC.*
Tel: 33(0)3 89 44 26 91

Created by the architect Vasconi, the spinning mill has become one of the Meccas of regional culture.

Situated around fifteen kilometres to the North of Mulhouse you find the 100 hectares Alsace's Ecomusée, it can be reached by bus (departure in front of Mulhouse Station). It is France's largest ecomusée and features some fifty Alsatian peasant houses, which have been removed from their villages of origin and set up here on the initiative of an association known as Maisons Paysannes d'Alsace. All types of houses are arranged according to their place of origin – Sundgau, Kochersberg, Ried etc, offering a complete panorama of the Alsatian habitat. Here the visitor can also meet artisans – blacksmith, sawyer, cartwright, clog-maker, baker – and watch them demonstrating their profession. An old lounge type manege – a beautiful example from the Belle Epoque - completes the tour of this open-air museum, which offers a very varied programme of activities throughout the year.

A Calium mine which you can ride in on a train completes the lively picture of life in the 19th and 20th century.

There are plans to extend the Alsace Ecomusée, France's largest open-air museum, in the near future.

Practical information.
Tel: 33(0)3 89 74 44 74, Tax: 33(0)3 89 74 44 65
contact@ecoparcs.com; www.ecomusee-alsace.com
Le Bioscope, Amusement Park. *BP 22, F-68190 Ungersheim*
Tel: 33(0)3 89 74 44 54. contact@lebioscope.com; www.lebioscope.com

Information

47 Sundgau

Altkirch

The old town of Altkirch is perched on a promontory overlooking of the River Ill. The main square is surrounded by the town hall, which was built in the 18th Century by Kléber, who was an architect prior to becoming a general in the Napoleonic army. Next to this, what was the former house of the seigneury's bailiff and is today the Sundgau Museum displays a rich collection of typical furniture as well as the works of Jean-Jacques Henner (1829-1905), a native of this region. In the centre of the square stands a Gothic fountain decorated with a statue of the Virgin, a vestige of the former Church of Notre-Dame. At the town's peak, the current Neoromanesque church stands on the site of the former château, built from the 11th Century by the ancestors of the Counts of Ferrette. Another attraction of this subprefecture, which used to be the seat of an important seigneury: the vestiges of the ramparts. The tourist office is situated in a 14th Century tower. A visit to a very well-known place of pilgrima-

Dubbed "Alsatian Switzerland", the region of Sundgau boasts peaceful countryside, houses with characteristic paintings that can be found nowhere else and romantic ruins.

Information

Tourist Office, 5, Place Xavier Jourdain, F-68130 Altkirch
Tel: 33(0)3 89 40 02 90 – Fax: 33(0)3 89 08 86 90
info@ot-altkirch.com; www.ot-altkirch.com
***Sundgau Museum**, Place de la République*
Tel: 33(0)3 89 40 00 04
Alsatian Jura Tourist Office,
Espace Mazarin, Rte de Lucelle à Ferrette
Tel: 33(0)3 89 08 23 88
***Musée Paysan**, 10, rue Principale, F-68480 Oltingue*
Tel: 33(0)3 89 40 79 24

ge, 1km from Altkirch, is highly recommended: the chapelle Saint Morand, patron saint of the town and its wine growers.

Ferrette and Oltingue

This pretty hilltop town has still retained its mediaeval appearance. It was the capital of the Alsatian territories of the Hapsburg dynasty. The local museum is situated in the 16th Century town hall, adorned with a pinnacle turret and the Hapsburg and earldom coat of arms. Linger at the place des Comtes and its fountain, as well as the so very typical rue Saint Bernard. A porch added in the 17th Century marks the entrance to the château with its 16th Century gate that you pass through to discover a surrounding wall tower. In the courtyard stand corner towers as well as vestiges of the keep. The sole remains of the main château are a well, the façade, part of the guardroom and a terrace that overhangs the countryside. On descending towards the flat part of Ferrette, one notices a number of entrance gates and architectural details where coats of arms abound. Among these beautiful residences, the maison du Bailli and its courtyard, as well as the maison Dîmière [tithe house] will catch your eye, as well as the half-timbered façades surrounding the place Mazarin. You should also pay a visit to the nearby Paysan d'Oltingue Museum with its collection of numerous objects from the daily life of Sundgau.

Caveau du Tonneau d'Or Restaurant · *33, rue Gilardoni Tel: 33(0)3 89 40 69 79*
Fromager Bernard Antony
17, rue de la Montagne Vieux Ferrette, Tel: 33(0)3 89 40 42 22 (1km North of Ferrette via the D432) Cheese ceremony in his stub [cellar] at the end of each week.

The Vineyard Route

The 120-km long Alsace vineyard route stretches between Marlhenheim and Thann and most of the time unfurls along the Piedmont of the Vosges. You can't miss the signs decorated with a logo representing a bunch of grapes and a glass of wine, of which the yellow and green colour makes it easily identifiable. It is difficult to resist the temptation to stop at each town or village. One visit is essential wherever you go: that of entering a wine grower's abode to step directly into the cellar after having crossed the large courtyard. In the depths of the cellar a joyful sight awaits the visitors: barrels, bottles and tables filled with "rutscherle", little bevelled glasses designed for

wine tasting. September and particularly October are particularly propitious months for a trip to one of France's oldest vineyards, which dates back to the Roman era. It produces more than one million hectolitres a year, a third of which are put aside for exportation.

Alsatian wines bear the name of their vines, four of which benefit from appellation d'origine contrôlée (AOC) which indicates the fact that they rank among France's greatest wines. These so-called "noble" vines are Riesling, often regarded as the King of Alsatian wines, Gewurztraminer, which literally means spiced Traminer – famous for its highly perfumed aroma, Muscat and Pinot gris. Other wines include Pinot noir, Vin rosé d'origine bourguignonne, the quality of which improves from year to year and, Pinot blanc otherwise known as Klevner or Auxerrois, Sylvaner and Chasselas. Edelzwicker, which is frequently on the menu in wine taverns, is none other than a mixture of different sorts of vines but has to include a "noble" vine to merit its name. Since the official decrees passed between 1975 and 1992, there has also been the appellation "Grands Crus d'Alsace", something from which 51 areas, spread out across forty-seven communes, benefit. If they are made from "noble" vines, the wines of these areas have the right to bear the name of the locality where their vineyard is situated followed by the appellation "Grand Cru" [Vintage] and the name of

The Vineyard Route, the most famous of many tourist round walks which combine cultural and gastronomic pleasures: view of Kientzheim in the High-Rhine. To visit: Its Vineyard and Alsace Wine museum.

their vine. These vintage wines must contain a minimal amount of alcohol in their must, their yield must not exceed 70 hl and they are submitted to obligatory tasting prior to any kind of marketing.

Only grapes from "noble" vines can be picked when they are overripe, from the end of November to the beginning of December, for the production of special wines which are known as vendanges tardives, the quality of which stands comparison with Sauterne's greatest vintage wines. Eiswein [ice wine] is even rarer as this is made from late vintage grapes which are harvested at less than 7°C. Champagne cremant is even more common in Alsace, mousseux that are produced according to the champagne

method and make up 30% of the French market for sparkling wines. To find out more about Alsatian wines it is recommended that you visit the Kientzheim Château where the Confrérie Saint-Etienne set up an Alsace Wine Museum.

France's most northern vineyard is situated in North Alsace. Here you can taste the wines at the Cleebourg cooperative, which include those produced in the surrounding communes, mainly from "noble" vines. An exclusively Lower Rhine vineyard route has developed around Strasbourg, which under the name of "Couronne d'or" [Golden Crown] traverses twenty-one communes that are well marked with a special logo.

Dine Divinely in France

Having completed a long journey in the midst of vineyards, passed through mediaeval gates opening onto fairytale villages, marvelled at the architectural riches of the towns, meandered along the mountain roads of the Massif of the Vosges, sooner or later the exquisite moment will come when you wonder: "But where are we going to dine?" And in gourmet Alsace where happiness is considered to be part of the pleasures of food, there certainly isn't a lack of choice, ranging from high class star-studded restaurants to cosy wine taverns or rustic farmhouse inns.

Often from generation to genera-

tion, the great houses maintain a widely renowned tradition: at the zenith of the gastronomic firmament: Haeberlin in Illhaeusern, Emile Jung at the "Crocodile" and Antoine Westermann at the Buerehiesel in Strasbourg unceasingly produced new creations, to offer inventive cuisine, making them into the region's best-known chefs. If a stop at one of their esta-

blishments proves to be memorable, crossing the simple threshold of one of the little wine taverns with picturesque names such as "Le Saint Sépulcre" ["The Holy Sepulchre"], "Le Clou" ["The Highlight"] or "Le Coin des Pucelles" ["Virgins' Corner"] can have a similar effect. A Lower Rhine institution, these wine bars, initially established to sell off the production of a wine grower, have prospered throughout the whole of Alsace. In the Higher Rhine region they are known as wistube and are frequently housed in deep cellars. But whatever the location, at ground or basement level, the spirit is the same: one comes to taste

Alsatian wine accompanied by one of the innumerable little pork dishes which are known as: Waedele or jarret de porc [pork knuckle], presskopf, hure de porc en gelée [pork brawn in jelly], schiffele or schiffala, palette de porc fumée [smoked pork platter], gfillter söymawe or Schwinemawe - stuffed pork stomach ... That is providing one doesn't prefer sausages with evocative names such as "Männerstolz" [Male Pride] or "Ver-

stecklter", a saveloy hidden underneath a Gruyère salad. Besides, this style of language is not just reserved for pork as the wine tavern is also the kingdom of tarte à l'oignon, [onion tart], bibeleskâs or fromage blanc [fromage frais] and escargots [snails]. The wine tavern's conviviality is legendary: here you are happy to share a table with your neighbour without first being introduced. The regulars are the only ones who keep themselves to themselves, gathered around the stammtisch [regulars' table] which tends to be close to the bar. And the quiet atmosphere at the beginning of the evening generally becomes increasingly noisy as the pitchers of white wine are emptied. Beerlovers meet up in the large brasseries and tackl generous portions of choucroute [sauerkraut]. This traditional dish sometimes takes on even more unusual forms when it has an Alsatian garnish, i.e. is served with lard [bacon], knacks, quenelles [seasoned meat or fish dumplings poached in water and served with sauce] and jambonneau [knuckle of ham]. A case in point is the marvellous sauerkraut with fish – a mediaeval tradition brought up-to-date by Guy-Pierre Baumann, the Alsatian, who in addition to his Parisian restaurants, reopened "La Maison Kammerzell" and "L'Alsace à Table" in Strasbourg, where he was the first to marry the taste of fermented cabbage with salmon or other fresh water fish.

Thus, many restaurant dishes are traditional family dishes that have been passed down from generation to generation; a case in point is

baeckeoffe, a stew with three kinds of meats marinated in white wine which is cooked in a large oblong Soufflenheim pottery tureen. This was systematically on the menu on

Mondays, washday. In fact, once the ingredients were gathered together, all that remained was to seal the lid with a little dough before bringing the dish to the village baker whose job it was to cook it. This is the origin of the name "Baeckeoffe". Another family custom is flammekueche or tarte flambée, made from dough covered with cream, bacon and onion. This special tart was combined with the baking of bread and made with the scraps of dough cooked in the already warm oven. The tradition has gradually spread to all the restaurants in Alsace where families gather together, most frequently on Sunday evenings, where the tarte is served on a wooden board and cut into several slices that everyone rolls between their fingers, it is the very image of sharing and conviviality.

These very widespread dishes also include several that remain more local specialities. Matelote de poissons [fish stew], for example, generally made from pikeperch, pike and eel and accompanied by fresh pasta is eaten on the banks of the Rhine. Carpe frite [fried carp] – pieces of fish coated in flour and cooked in oil like doughnuts is one of the specialities of Sundgau which has established a "route de la carpe frite" [fried carp route] with a succession of restaurants that serve this delicacy. Several restaurants devote themselves to the preparation of succulent Dampfnüdle or nouilles à la vapeur [sweet yeast dumplings] which can make up a whole meal from main course through to dessert.

However, you should go to route

des Crêtes if you want a slap-up marcaire meal, in one of the numerous farmhouse inns.

The manufacturers of munster – this very tasty cheese – serve a buffet supper for residents, sometimes in a gite with simple surroundings and sometimes well hidden in the midst of nature where the countryside is magnificent. Munster quiches

and potatoes with bacon, fromage frais laced with kirsch make up these appetising little treats which never taste better than in the Massif of the Vosges after a long hike.

The food with the most refined taste remains foie gras which is a traditional part of all festivals.

Strasbourg foie gras pâté was served for the first time at the table of the Marshal of Contades by an inspired cook by the name of Jean Pierre Clause. This cook had the idea to produce a pâté with whole goose livers, mixed with veal and chopped bacon. This was an outstanding success to the point where this Strasbourg foies gras pâté beca-

me an integral dish at the table of Louis XVI at Versailles. Later on, another cook, Nicolas François Doyen, a native of Périgord, came to seek his fortune at Strasbourg and had the idea to add truffles to this recipe, which gave it a certain degree of refinement. As for this little story, it is curious to note that although today foie gras is served as an entrée, this exaltation of the tastebuds was in olden times consumed at the end of a meal. The rich composition of menus of centuries past leads one to think that our ancestors were very healthy!

Events

January
European Forum of Antiques and Art in Strasbourg

February
START Contemporary Art Exhibition in Strasbourg Tourissimo, Tourism Exhibition.

March
Carnival in several towns, including Strasbourg
Passion Plays in Masevaux including Strasbourg,
www.strasbourg.fr

May
Muguet Festival in Neuf-Brisach
Asparagus Festival in Hoerdt
Book Fair in Saint-Louis
Alsatian Post Card Fair in Pfaffenhoffen
Beltaine in Dambach-La-Ville
Festival of St Urban in Kintzheim
International ladies tennis cup (Strasbourg)

April
Snail Festival in Osenbach
Vinogast in Ammerschwihr
Eurobière Beer Festival in Strasbourg (odd years)

June
Corpus Christi procession in Geispolsheim
Kougelhopf Fair in Ribeauvillé
Folklore festival in Hunspach
Rose Festival in Saverne
Cremation of the Three Fir Trees in Thann
International Music Festival in Strasbourg
Mineral Market at Sainte-Marie-aux-mines

July

International Music Festival in Colmar

Great Automobile Parade in Mulhouse

Witch's Festival in Rouffach

Barr Wine Fair

Ami Fritz [Friend Fritz] Festival in Hunawihr

"Streisselhochzeit" – traditional marriage with bouquet in Seebach

August

Colmar Wine Fair

Gewürztraminer Festival in Bergheim

Stork Festival in Eguisheim

Marriage of Friend Fritz in Marlenheim

Procession of floral floats in Sélestat

"S'Wielada" – wine filling according to the old tradition in Zellenberg

Bilberry Festival in Wildenstein

Hops Festival in Haguenau

Moon Festival in Kogenheim

September

European Fair in Strasbourg

Musica, contemporary music festival in Strasbourg

Strolling clowns festival in Ribeauvillé

Pottery Festival in Betschdorf and Soufflenheim

International Bugatti Festival in Molsheim

New Wine Festival in Saint-Hippolyte

October

Grape harvest festival in Barr

Grape harvest festival in Obernai

Pie Festival in Munster

Pumpkin Festival in Logelheim

New Wine Festival in Eguisheim

European nights in Strasbourg

International Beer Fair in Strasbourg

November
Venison Festival in Ranspach-Le-Bas Beginning of Christmas markets in Strasbourg, Colmar and Andlau

December
The whole of Alsace celebrates Christmas, many markets, particularly in:
Wissemberg, Haguenau, Obernai, Lolsheim, Barr, Sélestat, Ribeauvillé, Kaysersberg, Colmar, Mulhouse, etc.Special leaflet in all tourist offices, information centres and townhalls.

Strasbourg, Christmas Capital

Legend: Alsace Overview Map

10	Chapter number
☿ ♂	Church/chapel,Palace/castle
A4	Motorway
N62	main road
	other road
	railway
—··—··—	border